LIBRARIES,

LEADERSHIP,

AND SCHOLARLY

COMMUNICATION

LIBRARIES, LEADERSHIP, AND SCHOLARLY COMMUNICATION

Essays by
RICK ANDERSON

An imprint of the American Library Association

CHICAGO | 2016

Extensive effort has gone into ensuring the reliability of the information in this book; however, the publisher makes no warranty, express or implied, with respect to the material contained herein.

ISBNs
978-0-8389-1433-5 (paper)
978-0-8389-1442-7 (PDF)
978-0-8389-1443-4 (ePub)
978-0-8389-1444-1 (Kindle)

Library of Congress Cataloging-in-Publication Data

Names: Anderson, Rick, 1965– author.
Title: Libraries, leadership, and scholarly communication / essays by Rick Anderson.
Description: Chicago : ALA Editions, an imprint of the American Library Association, 2016. | Includes bibliographical references and index.
Identifiers: LCCN 2015049392| ISBN 9780838914335 (paper : alk. paper) | ISBN 9780838914427 (PDF) | ISBN 9780838914434 (ePub) | ISBN 9780838914441 (Kindle)
Subjects: LCSH: Academic libraries—Aims and objectives. | Research libraries—Aims and objectives. | Academic libraries—Collection development. | Research libraries--Collection development. | Libraries and publishing. | Communication in learning and scholarship.
Classification: LCC Z675.U5 A5935 2016 | DDC 027.7--dc23 LC record available at http://lccn.loc.gov/2015049392

Cover design by Kimberly Thornton. Cover image © Shutterstock, Inc.
Text design and composition by Adrianna Sutton in the Scala and Scala Sans typefaces.

♾ This paper meets the requirements of ANSI/NISO Z39.48–1992 (Permanence of Paper).

Printed in the United States of America

20 19 18 17 16   5 4 3 2 1

This book is gratefully dedicated to everyone who has argued with me, whether publicly or privately, over the issues discussed in these essays. Thanks for keeping me on my toes.

·

But mostly it's dedicated to my wonderful, patient wife, Laura, who also keeps me on my toes.

CONTENTS

PREFACE

AS MANY OF MY COLLEAGUES have noticed—with varying mixtures of amusement, pleasure, alarm, and disgust—I write a lot.

The main reason for this is that I'm too scatterbrained and unfocused to think about things. I try, but I can't do it; as soon as I start pondering, I immediately get distracted by e-mail, other people, music, iPhone Scrabble, squirrels, the need to trim my nails, or just other, more interesting thoughts. In order to think about something I have to do one of three things: run, talk, or write. And of those three, writing is the one most likely to result in something concretely useful. The problem with running is that I get good ideas while I'm doing it, but I forget them by the time I get home. The problem with talking is that my colleagues always seem to be "busy" doing "work," and my wife's patience with library shoptalk is, apparently, limited. So if an issue or a problem catches my interest and I want to work through its implications, the most effective (and considerate) way for me to do so is to open up a Word document and start typing. It feels a little bit like sitting down with a wadded-up tangle of string and slowly pulling the wad apart until it's straight. Usually, about 1,500 words later, I've figured out what I think about that thing—and, sometimes, those 1,500 words will turn out to be something that an editor believes other people will want to read.

This process has resulted in thousands of written products over the past twenty-five years that have been published in a variety of manifestations: columns, reviews, opinion essays, articles, white papers, blog postings, etc. And as I went through them to find items for inclusion in this book, I looked for patterns—patterns in the topics that I've covered, in the arguments I've made, and in the ideas and underlying concerns that have emerged as recurring themes.

One thing I noticed is that I seem to be drawn generally toward the idea of forced choices, and the ways in which being required to choose tends to result in conflict, both within ourselves as individuals (as we struggle to reconcile our own competing priorities and desires) and

xi

between us as colleagues (as we try to distribute money, time, energy, and space in support of important programs and projects). Anyone who reads these essays is going to encounter the concepts of forced choices and conflicting values, in various guises, over and over again. Why is that?

Some of it probably has to do with the fact that I'm the oldest child of a large family. And as anyone who has lived with one can tell you, we oldest children tend to have a thing about rules. One of the rules is this: if you have strictly limited resources, you have to make choices. And whenever you're forced to make choices, values are going to come into conflict: it's at the point of unavoidable choice-making that the argument "But X is a good thing!" is no longer sufficient to carry the day because Y and Z are good things too, and yet we don't have enough money or time or space or energy to do all three of them.

This is the point at which I start getting really interested. Questions like "Do people love the library?" and "Does intellectual freedom matter?" and "Should everyone have free access to scholarly information?" are not interesting to me because the correct answer to such questions is so trivially obvious that, really, the only reason I can imagine for even asking them is if we're looking for an excuse to congratulate ourselves. Much more interesting to me are questions like these:

> "How much time and energy are our patrons demonstrably willing to expend in order to use the library?"
> "What are we, as librarians, willing to give up in order for our patrons (and our colleagues) to have meaningful intellectual freedom?"
> "How much does it cost to make scholarly information freely available to the public, and who should pay—and by what mechanisms?"

Each of those questions requires us to deal with the concept of cost, which is another way of saying "forced choice." If we have two options, one of which is objectively and demonstrably bad and the other of which is objectively and demonstrably good, then there probably won't be much conflict in the choice-making—all of us prefer good things over bad ones. Difficulty arises when both options are good and we can't have both.

Whenever we, as members of an organization like a library, are forced to choose between good things, we may start by trying to figure out some way to have both things. But in many cases, that will turn out to be impossible and we'll have to decide which good thing is going to take priority over the other. We can't make that decision without invoking values, and the moment we start invoking values is when the conversation can take a really difficult and interesting turn. In a market-driven organization there's a powerful, built-in incentive to confront these questions and resolve them quickly—because if you don't, you'll go out of business. But in mission-driven organizations like libraries there's a powerful, built-in incentive to gloss over such questions and pretend they aren't real—because confronting them requires you to deal with the painful truth that not everyone in the organization has the same priorities and wants the same things in the same amounts.

And this brings me to the issue of provocation and controversy. Some years back, a somewhat well-known member of the library commentariat collared me in the hallway at a conference and asked me something startling. I don't remember his exact words, but the gist of his question was this: "The stuff you write and say in meetings is just to provoke, right? You don't really mean any of it, do you?"

I was so taken aback by the question that I honestly don't remember exactly how I answered it. I'm afraid that I probably said something conciliatory and reassuring. If I did, then I was being less than fully honest, and I figure now is as good a time as any to set the record straight.

The truth is that I would never write or say something just to provoke a reaction, or even just to spur a different kind of thinking. I'm not interested in provocation for the sake of provocation. If I say something in writing or in a public talk, I mean it, and I'm willing to stand behind it. In the years that have passed since that encounter in the hallway, I've often wished I'd had the presence of mind and the guts to say that in the moment.

This doesn't mean that I believe I'm always right, of course, and there may well be things I've said in the past that I would disavow today. But I meant them when I said them and continued to mean them until I was convinced otherwise or until circumstances changed sufficiently to alter my position. (In fact, several of the essays in this collection have been edited to reflect changes in my thinking since they were originally published.)

The reality is that I have no particular interest in being provocative, nor am I very interested in preserving tradition or being innovative, in promoting group solidarity or championing uniqueness, in being a good doobie or being a rebel.

What does interest me very much is *seeing things as they really are*. I make no claim to being better at this than anyone else is—but wanting to see things as they really are is what interests me and what drives me to write and speak. It's what drives me to think hard about issues that seem important, and to say what I believe is really true. If what seems to me to be true doesn't sound particularly innovative, or if it sounds provocative, or if it goes against tradition, or if it supports tradition, I'm fine with that. When it comes to library practices, I care about what works—but, of course, you can't figure out what works unless you know what you're trying to do, and you can't figure out what you're going to try to do unless you set priorities, and you can't set priorities without invoking values, and now we're back to those difficult conversations again.

Difficult Conversations was actually one of the candidates for a title to this book. But I rejected it because I don't want to focus on "difficulty"; I want to focus on figuring out what's true and what works. My hope is that these essays have made, and will continue to make, some contribution to that effort.

SECTION I

LIBRARIES AND THEIR COLLECTIONS, NOW AND IN THE FUTURE

1

Being Essential Is Not Enough

IS THERE ANY APPLAUSE LINE in our profession more tried-and-true than the assertion that "libraries are essential"? It comes in multiple forms, all of them familiar: "Libraries are the cornerstone of democracy"; "The library is the heart of the campus"; "Libraries are rungs on the ladder of opportunity"; etc.

The problem with such statements is not that they're wrong. In fact, arguments supporting the idea that "libraries are essential"—whether to the academy or to society generally—vary in quality. Some of them are stronger, some are weaker. But there is a problem with all of them, and the problem is that they pose a danger. To the degree that we, as librarians, take them to heart, they all threaten to leave us complacent about our future. What will determine our future is not whether we and our services are *essential in fact*, but whether we are seen by our stakeholders as *more essential than the other essential programs and projects that are competing for the same resources.*

To put it more simply: being essential is no guarantee of survival. Essential things are lost every day.

Consider the federal budget sequestration crisis of 2013. The sequestration proposal, with its automatic and massive budget cuts, was conceived as a kind of "nuclear option," a budget-cutting scenario so odious that the threat of it would force all legislative parties to the negotiating table in order to avoid its implementation. Before it was implemented, many observers would have said that the things it threatened to cut were "essential"—education funding, military readiness, disaster relief—and, arguably, those observers would have been correct. And yet the cuts happened anyway—not because the things that were cut

---

This essay was originally published as two columns in *Library Journal*'s *Academic Newswire*, June 5 and July 10, 2014. Reprinted by permission.

turned out not to be essential after all, but because being "essential" is no guarantee of safety.

Here's a hard truth to which I think we, in academic libraries, pay far too little attention, either because we don't believe it's true or because its truth is too painful for us to consider: academic libraries, as we know them, do not have to stay in business. Here's an even harder truth: no library *should* stay in business if it fails to give reasonable value in return for the huge amount of campus resources it consumes.

On every campus, the library represents an enormous institutional investment—in some cases, it is the institution's single most expensive program. Yet, unlike many of the schools and departments into which the university sinks far less of its strictly limited resources, the library usually brings in relatively little (if any) external funding or other kinds of outside support. It takes and takes and takes, and what it gives back is intangible and difficult to assess and quantify.

Does the fact that the library's outputs are intangible and hard to measure mean that we don't, in fact, return good value? Absolutely not. What we do is arguably important, even "essential," and we often make that argument articulately and persuasively. But in a higher-education environment characterized by scarce resources, we have to do more than just convince people of the fact that we're needed.

The core problem we face is that on every campus, the number of arguably essential programs, projects, and capital purchases far outstrips the resources available to support them. Laboratories, classrooms, water and electrical systems, scholarship programs, and faculty recruitment are all essential, and all are competing for the same pool of university resources (which includes not only money but also space, administrative attention, and staff time). Essentialness is good at attracting dollars when dollars are available; it is not good at making dollars appear out of thin air.

Let's consider some of the implications of that reality.

Put yourself in the position of a provost or vice president who is charged with allocating $1 million across the various academic programs and infrastructural needs on her campus. One possible approach would be to divide up the $1 million by simply giving 20 programs $50,000 each. This approach would be easy, and would have the superficial appearance of fairness, but in most cases I believe it would be irresponsible.

The provost's job is not to make sure that every program gets equal treatment, but rather to make sure that the university's mission is being accomplished. No college or university focuses equally on every discipline; some focus more on the humanities and social sciences, others on applied sciences. Some have a stronger outreach mission, others are more dedicated to international programs. The provost's job is to figure out how to use that $1 million to move the university forward as effectively as possible. Depending on what "forward" means for that particular university, it may be that half of the money should go to the library; maybe 90 percent of it should go to scholarships.

In my experience, campus leaders tend to understand this intuitively and rarely distribute money evenly; instead, they try to distribute it in ways that mirror the mission of the university. That's why, if the library wants not only to be *called* "essential" but also to be *treated as if it is essential*, it had better be aligning itself with that mission—and doing so explicitly, visibly, and effectively.

What might some examples of that kind of alignment look like?

Let me begin by bragging about my own boss. When it came time to submit a budget request recently, our dean and university librarian, Alberta Comer, did not simply write a letter describing all the wonderful and worthwhile things the library does, followed by a request for additional support. Instead, she worked with her leadership team to create a two-part document: the first section outlined the library's significant achievements over the past year, and the second explained what we want to do in the coming year. Importantly, each of those sections was organized according to the university's explicitly expressed programmatic priorities. Thus, the message our vice president received was not "Here are all the reasons why you ought to give the library more money." Instead, it was "Here are some of the most important ways in which the library is moving the university toward its goals, and here are ways in which we could do that even better if we had more resources to work with."

The result was clear success. Although we certainly didn't get everything we asked for, the new allocation of recurring and one-time funds we did receive represented a disproportionately large share of what was available for distribution across campus. This is the takeaway lesson: map your library's programs and services to the mission of the university and you will be seen as an essential strategic partner, not just another piece of costly infrastructure. (Thanks to Yale University Librarian Susan Gibbons, who beautifully articulated this point during a conversation I had with her.)

Speaking of Yale, another great example of this kind of alignment comes from that university's Harvey Cushing/John Hay Whitney Medical Library, which has created, not only course modules that are designed specifically to help the medical school achieve the goals of its Graduate Medical Education program, but also courses (in multiple versions) in evidence-based practice for the nursing school and, according to the library's interim director, John Gallagher, a program to help medical faculty and researchers comply with the National Institutes of Health's open-access policies. This last point suggests a second takeaway lesson: solving a problem that already exists for your faculty and has a tangible impact on their daily work (such as compliance with a mandate) is more likely to generate support for the library than trying to convince the faculty that they have a problem.

A third library organization that shines in this regard is the one at North Carolina State University. Seeing that its university was adopting a program of faculty cluster hiring in support of its overarching goal to "enhance interdisciplinary scholarship to address the grand challenges of society," associate dean Greg Raschke reports that the library system "is aligning its efforts across a spectrum of areas to foster the success of the clusters." These efforts include adapting existing collection-analysis tools to ensure that they map to the interdisciplinary clusters, offering dedicated collaboration space for use by faculty working in those clusters, reaching out to the clusters with targeted information about existing technology offerings in the libraries, and "providing dedicated subject specialists for each faculty cluster to work across the life-cycle of their research to offer guidance and connections to services such as visualization, GIS support, copyright guidance, bibliometric analysis, research data management, research funding tools, and collections." Here is the third takeaway lesson: sometimes aligning your library with institutional goals and programs means creating new services, and sometimes it means adapting old ones. Since our host institutions are always changing, it always means responding quickly and nimbly to new programs and priority shifts.

What can each of us do at our own institutions? Here are a few general guidelines:

- *Listen to your president and your provost.* And not just for obvious points of connection between what your campus leaders say and what the library traditionally does (student success, research impact, etc.). Listen also for areas of emphasis that you might not think of as relevant to the library. If the president says that one of her chief areas of concern is improving the six-year graduation rate, don't dismiss that as having nothing to do with the library—ask yourself what the library might do differently (or what it might already be doing) that could have an impact on that goal, even if the goal doesn't seem to be connected directly to library services.

- *Monitor your university's public pronouncements, press releases, tweets, etc., and see what is said most often.* It's not just what your campus leaders and spokespersons say but how often and in how many contexts they say it that will tip you off to a particularly important or emerging area of institutional focus. If words and phrases like "applied research," "diversity," "international," "sustainability," "commercial partnerships," or "community impact" are repeatedly appearing in your university's public pronouncements, speeches, and press releases, you're getting a message. This is especially key for public colleges and universities, where everything that's said publicly is said with the keen understanding that lawmakers and other fiscal officers are listening. Ask yourself what your institution says when it knows the people who hold the purse strings are listening—then ask yourself how your library can help the institution make its case.
- *Become intimately familiar with your institution's strategic plan and its mission and vision statements.* These documents describe the programmatic skeleton that underlies everything your university is doing. If the library is doing things that don't help further the goals and strategies laid out in them, ask yourself why—and unless the answers you come up with are unusually compelling and can be defended (with a straight face) in conversation with your provost or vice president, seriously consider discontinuing them. If your library is doing things that actively undermine those goals and strategies, stop doing those things immediately. As you consider establishing new programs or practices in your library, ask yourself from the very beginning how those new programs or practices will help further the strategic mission of your institution.
- *Watch the curriculum, and don't confuse equality with fairness.* This is something that all academic libraries understand in principle, but we sometimes struggle with it in practice because its application is painful: no library that aligns itself to institutional priorities will end up serving all programs and all academic disciplines equally. This is true because no college or university places an equal strategic emphasis on every discipline and program. What this means is that our budgets and programmatic support should not be distributed equally

across disciplines but should reflect the curricular and strategic emphases of our host institutions. And since academic institutions rarely come right out and say, "We care more about physics than we do about astronomy," this means your monitoring of institutional communications for strategic hints will have to be sensitive to nuance and informed by an awareness of how other campus resources are distributed.

2

My Name Is Ozymandias, King of Kings

THE OTHER DAY I read a kind of fascinating dissection of the performance of Yahoo CEO Marissa Mayer during her first two years at the helm of that company.[1] The analysis of her decisions (both good and bad) was interesting to me in and of itself. As usual when reading an article about organizations dealing with radical change in their environments, I also looked for lessons I could derive for leadership in libraries, and—also as usual—I was getting the incredibly frustrating feeling that those lessons were there to be seen but I was failing to see them. Then came the final two paragraphs, which I will discuss separately:

> In many ways, Yahoo's decline from a $128 billion company to one worth virtually nothing is entirely natural. Yahoo grew into a colossus by solving a problem that no longer exists. And while Yahoo's products have undeniably improved, and its culture has become more innovative, it's unlikely that Mayer can reverse an inevitability unless she creates the next iPod. All breakthrough companies, after all, will eventually plateau and then decline. U.S. Steel was the first billion-dollar company in 1901, but it was worth about the same in 1991. Kodak, which once employed nearly 80,000 people, now has a market value below $1 billion. Packard and Hudson ruled the roads for more than 40 years before disappearing. These companies matured and receded over the course of generations, in some cases even a century. Yahoo went through the process in 20 years. In the technology industry, things move fast.

This essay was originally published in *The Scholarly Kitchen* (blog), January 7, 2015.

Three things struck me immediately about these observations.

First and most obviously, the fact that *even mighty corporate entities will eventually fall*, no matter how invincible they seem today. (In Percy Bysshe Shelley's famous poem, two monumental carved legs stand alone in the Egyptian desert, surrounded by sand, "boundless and bare." By their feet is inscribed "My name is Ozymandias, King of Kings / Look on my works, ye mighty, and despair.")

Second, *the irrelevance of past performance to future performance when everything about the context in which you're performing has changed.* Being the best in the world at something that hardly anyone wants you to do any longer is a losing strategy, regardless of how much everyone in the world wanted you to do it twenty or ten years ago—or two years ago, or one—and regardless of whether or not we all agree that the thing you're doing is good or admirable. Sometimes people don't want you to do that thing anymore because they no longer care (rightly or wrongly) about the thing itself; sometimes they no longer want you to do it because someone else is doing that thing decisively better. And here, of course, is a lesson for research libraries: for at least a century, the library as traditionally understood was the Ozymandias that bestrode the world of information-seeking; in 1950 (or 1990, for that matter), despite the warnings of fevered futurists, it was hard to take seriously the idea of the world bypassing the library, consistently and systematically, in the search for information. Then things changed, very suddenly and very radically, and it is now difficult to take seriously the idea of most people beginning their research process within the walls (either physical or virtual) of a library. Most—virtually all—research begins with a Web search, as of course it should in order to be effective. For people who need information, this represents an enormous advance in quality of life. For research libraries, this represents a crisis—maybe a relatively slow-moving one, but a decisive, fundamental, and systemic one.

The third thing that struck me about the paragraph above was more disturbing than the first two, however, perhaps because it's a long-standing problem that came into focus for me only when I read this article: it's *the ease with which we, in libraries, have been able to convince ourselves that we're operating in anything but a technology industry.* We don't like either of those words: "technology" or "industry." "Industry" implies that we're trying to make money, which of course we really are not; we exist to spend it. As for "technology": Sure, we talk a good game about being early adopters and about embracing technological change, but when we talk like that we're kidding ourselves. Librarianship (almost as much as scholarly publishing) is a radically reactionary profession, and I can't think of a single innovation—technological or otherwise—that we have actively embraced at the time that it appeared. I think it would be more accurate to say that the world has, in a number of ways, successfully dragged us, kicking and screaming, out of the nineteenth century and into the twentieth. Unfortunately, of course, we're well into the twenty-first century. (The fact that at the beginning of 2015, we have only just adopted a new machine-readable cataloging standard—the old one having been created in the mid-1960s—should maybe alarm us a bit more than it does.) When we talk publicly about technological change in libraries, it's too often in one of two ways: either we're patting ourselves on the back for being so ready to embrace it, or we're talking about how a particular technological change doesn't really apply to us. But the information world has become, decisively and whether we like it or not, a technology industry. Certainly in the global north (and across large swaths of the global south as well, including many of the most impoverished areas), digital networks are the primary means by which information is shared. Books are still *read* in print and likely will be for a very long time; but in the developed world, a relatively small and shrinking number of people turn to ink on paper in order to *gather information*.

Here, of course, is where I issue my standard disclaimer: doing new things in new ways isn't an unalloyed good in and of itself, and it's true that some of the real value libraries have always offered, and that we continue to offer, lies in the fact that we preserve old things—notably documents, in a variety of formats and manifestations. The problem, I think, is that we have come to confuse the importance of our role as conservators of documents with a mandate to conserve library practices and culture. There is indeed something sacred about making documents permanently available; however, there's nothing whatsoever sacred about any particular workflow or technology we use in pursuit of that goal. Confusing the sacredness of ends with the sacredness of means is one symptom of a disease that could easily kill us.

All of that being said, consider this final paragraph from the article on Marissa Mayer and Yahoo:

"Sometimes," Damodaran told me, "companies have to act their age." For Yahoo, embracing its maturity means settling for a business that earns close to $1 billion in profit every year. It has outlasted other formerly iconic Internet portals, from AltaVista to Excite, and even dwarfs more recent web sensations like Myspace and Ask.com. For a company that started out as "Jerry and David's Guide to the World Wide Web," that's not a bad way to grow old.

I have to confess that sometimes dangerous and unwelcome thoughts pop into my mind. Sometimes these thoughts come in the form of a monologue between one part of my brain, the troublemaking part, and the other. The troublemaking part says something like this:

> Instead of trying to turn into something radically different from what we once were in order to stay big and well-funded and centrally relevant, we in libraries should simply let time and the tide of change have their way with us. If our traditional services are no longer centrally important, maybe we should be content with retaining marginal relevance. There are worse things than being a niche player, if you're a good one. Maybe the faculty librarians who retire will be replaced by technical staff, or not replaced at all. Maybe, as the usage of our physical collections continues to decline, more and more of the shelves that contain those collections will be removed to make space for academic advising offices, or group study spaces, or makerspaces or multimedia production labs. Certainly if open access becomes the predominant model of scholarly publishing, as its advocates hope and anticipate it will (and sometimes claim it already has), it will become much more difficult to justify multimillion-dollar collections budgets—but if we lose collections budgets because high-quality scholarly information has become freely accessible, in what sense could that possibly be called a bad thing for scholarship? Should the library "industry" simply "embrac[e] its maturity" and "act [its] age"?

Let me be clear, because I fully expect that the provocative things I just said in the above paragraph will be quoted out of the context of their qualifying bracketing statements: I try not to entertain the thoughts I just summarized above because I don't think they're constructive. And I'm certainly not advocating an erosion in the importance and centrality of research libraries, nor by any means am I calling on myself and my colleagues to sit back and enjoy the ride to the margins of academic life.

But here's a thought experiment that I do think is useful: Suppose the research library were, in fact, to move to the margins of academic life on my campus—its budget massively cut, its spaces substantially taken over by other campus entities, its faculty and staff decimated. How would the negative impact of that change be felt in the day-to-day lives of my university's students and faculty? The answer to that question, it seems to me, is the answer to the question "How is my library making a difference to its sponsoring institution?"—and that seems to me to be about as existentially important a question as can be asked of us (and by us) at this point in our history.

NOTE

1. Nicholas Carson, "No Results," *The New York Times Magazine* (December 2014): 22–27, 44–46.

3

The Crisis in Research Librarianship

THE ACADEMIC RESEARCH LIBRARY, as currently configured, is designed and organized to solve a problem that its patrons no longer perceive: the problem of information scarcity.

When information is scarce, it presents two primary difficulties: first, it may be hard to find; second, it is expensive. These may seem like trivial observations, but they go to the heart of a growing crisis in librarianship. The crisis does not stem from the fact that information is now universally cheap and easy to find, and therefore that librarians are no longer needed; on the contrary, some kinds of information (high-quality science publications, for example) are still expensive, and some (including unique documents like manuscripts and gray literature) are still difficult to find. In the face of these and other persistent information problems (such as the difficulty of distinguishing between authoritative and questionable sources), librarians continue to offer valuable help in their roles as brokers and as research guides.

So the problem is not that libraries fail to offer value to their constituents. The crisis stems, instead, from the following three facts:

First, *perception matters more than reality*. To be more precise: the future of libraries will not be determined by the degree to which libraries offer genuine value to their patrons; it will be determined by the actual behavior of their patrons, and patron behavior is shaped only partially by the real value of library services. If patrons believe that they have free access to all of the information products they need, and if they believe that they are fully capable of finding those products and using them effectively without help, and if they act on those beliefs, the effect on libraries will be exactly the same whether those beliefs are correct or

This essay was originally published in the *Journal of Academic Librarianship* 37, no. 4 (2011): 290. Reprinted by permission.

incorrect. Furthermore, trying to convince patrons that they are wrong in their beliefs will, except in rare and isolated cases, be a losing battle; patrons' persistent confidence in their self-sufficiency as information users has been amply documented, most recently in the OCLC report *Perceptions of Libraries, 2010: Context and Community.*[1]

Second, *patrons genuinely do not need librarians as much as they once did*. Although it is true that some kinds of information products remain expensive and difficult to find, this is no longer true of most kinds of information products—even very high-quality ones. This reality has snuck up on us. For centuries, the only way to find reliable factual data and high-quality scholarly publications was to travel to a library and ask a librarian for help. The decline in the number of people willing to do this—at least in research libraries—over the past fifteen years has been staggering: according to Association of Research Library (ARL) statistics, the number of reference transactions taking place in ARL libraries has declined by more than half since 1995.[2] Control that statistic for enrollment and the decline is greater: in 1995, ARL libraries provided an average of 10.1 reference transactions per student FTE; in 2009 the number was 3.6, a decline of over 60 percent. Such statistics strongly suggest (though do not prove) that patrons are finding information effectively without help; at the very least, they support the proposition mentioned above—that patrons largely and increasingly consider themselves fully capable of doing so. While surveys designed to measure the affection and respect in which libraries are held among the general public continue to provide heartwarming results, the actual behavior of patrons in research libraries points to a more sobering reality.

Third, *value that is not valued is not valuable*. In the marketplace, the value of a consumer good (such as a car or a toaster) is determined entirely by the consumer. A toaster company may make a value proposition ("Manufacturer's suggested retail price: $39.99"), but unless customers agree with that proposition in sufficient numbers, it is meaningless: a product is worth only what buyers are willing to pay for it. As librarians, we pride ourselves on operating outside of the commercial marketplace. However, whether we like it or not, we are working in an information environment the dynamics of which are very much like those of a free market, except that the currency spent by our "customers" is not money, but time and attention. We procure for our patrons products (books, articles, etc.) and offer services (bibliographic instruction, one-on-one research guidance, etc.) that we believe are valuable, and our patrons choose whether or not to invest time in our offerings based on the value they expect to gain from doing so. We may believe, for example, that our carefully crafted catalog records provide excellent value in return for the time and energy required to use them—and we may be right. But if our patrons doubt that the catalog will return good value in exchange for the time and energy required to use it, then whatever value the catalog may actually contain becomes irrelevant. Nor, as Karen Calhoun explained in her monumental study *The Changing Nature of the Catalog and Its Integration with Other Discovery Tools*, does the catalog's value necessarily increase as we increase our investment in it.[3] This same principle applies to virtually all library services just as it does to consumer goods in the commercial marketplace.

What are the implications of these three realities, and how have they contributed to the current crisis in research libraries?

Although libraries have moved their products and services (with varying degrees of willingness at first, but now generally with enthusiasm) into the digital environment in which virtually all information-seeking now takes place, we hold many of our traditional organizational structures, practices, and mind-sets in an increasingly desperate death grip. It has taken us a very long time to realize, for example, that an e-journal is not just a print journal in a different format; it is a different animal entirely. For many of us, it remains difficult to acknowledge that even in the print environment, books were more often used as databases than as texts for extended linear reading (regardless of what their authors may have intended or wanted). And we continue to view the comprehensive and well-crafted library collection as an end in itself.

Meanwhile, our competitors in the marketplace of time and attention have not been saddled with the same legacy of assumptions: Google comprehended quickly that for researchers, much of the value of a printed book lies in its usefulness as a database, and acted accordingly to turn millions of printed books into e-books, thus making them much more effective as databases. *Wikipedia* is founded on the belief (largely correct, as it turns out) that crowds both can and will provide high-quality content and metadata to the world at no charge. For our part, in research libraries, we still tend to treat books as if they are primarily tools for linear reading, and metadata records as artisanal products. We still build collections that are fenced off from the larger information world and encourage our patrons, against all reason, to begin their information searches within the confines of our artificially limited collections.

What is the crisis? It consists of the fact that so many of the functions and structures to which we cling play such a marginal role in the real lives of our patrons. Virtually none of them begin a research project at the library's website; the average student at a major research university has fewer than four interactions with a reference librarian in a year (and few of those are substantive reference interviews); printed books circulate at lower and lower rates every year. Students continue to use our libraries in droves, but primarily because libraries often provide the most spacious, comfortable, and well-equipped study space on campus. Offering a better and more academically serious version of the student union is not a bad thing—but by continuing to invest very large portions of our time, energy, and budget in services that are of decreasing value to our clientele at the same time that our sponsoring institutions are coming under increasingly desperate financial pressure, we run the serious risk of having our missions pulled out from under us.

Can the research library go out of business? Yes. What might "going out of business" look like? Like any other death, it can take a variety of forms. Some symptoms of possibly terminal decline might include the following:

- As information becomes more and more divorced from physical formats, campus administrators see less and less of a meaningful distinction between the library and general campus information technology infrastructure; library directors' reporting lines begin shifting from provosts to CFOs or CIOs, and the directors themselves are eventually replaced by IT administrators. Retiring librarians are replaced, not by new librarians, but by information technologists.
- Improvements in both hardware and software make laptops and handheld devices ubiquitous, powerful, and versatile enough that large computer labs become obsolete, robbing libraries of a significant percentage of their users even as reference transactions and circulation of physical materials continue their precipitous declines.
- Continued budget pressure leads campus administrators to investigate more rigorously the return on investment of library budgets (especially materials budgets) and to find that investment—rightly or wrongly—less cost-effective than, for example, the construction of new classroom buildings or refurbishment of aging lab facilities.
- Libraries begin to disappear by erosion: intralibrary units such as knowledge commons, instruction labs, and classroom facilities are gradually taken over by other campus entities—or other campus entities simply take over library space themselves.

Eventually, the term "library" becomes an honorific attached to a building, rather than a meaningful designation for what happens inside it.

- The library's brokerage function is obviated. Imagine this scenario: The library refuses, with good reason, to renew a restrictive and financially unsustainable e-journal package subscription. In response, the publisher goes directly to individual faculty members, offering them individual access to the same package at a very low individual subscription rate. If that sounds unrealistic given the costs of such retail selling, consider the publisher's alternative if the library cannot afford to continue its subscription: no sale at all.

Today, the research library is at an inflection point. Unfortunately, it is easy to ignore that fact. Although many libraries are suffering budget cuts along with other campus entities, there is in most places little direct evidence of a coming crisis of support. We continue to enjoy the respect (and sometimes even the veneration) of faculty and administration, and support for the library is still invoked somberly as a bedrock principle of academic seriousness. But the foundation on which that support is built has eroded over the past two decades: supporting the library in the old ways (primarily by funding the amassing of large but still fatally limited collections selected according to librarians' speculations about future needs, and by hiring large faculties of librarians whose services are decreasingly demanded by researchers) is not sustainable in the current environment. Unless we give our sponsoring institutions better and more compelling reasons to support libraries, they will be forced by economic reality to stop doing so—or to stop doing so in the ways they always have. We must look with cold and hardheaded rationality at our current practices and ask ourselves not *what value they offer* but, rather, *what value our patrons believe they offer.* If what we offer our patrons is not perceived as valuable by them, then we have two choices: change their minds, or redirect our resources. The former is virtually impossible; the latter is enormously painful. But the latter is possible, and if we do not undertake such a redirection ourselves, it will almost certainly be undertaken for us.

NOTES

1.   OCLC, *Perceptions of Libraries, 2010: Context and Community* (Dublin, OH: OCLC, 2011), www.oclc.org/reports/2010perceptions.en.html.

2. Association of Research Libraries, "ARL Statistics and Salary Surveys," www.arl.org/stats/annualsurveys/arlstats/index.shtml.

3. Karen Calhoun, *The Changing Nature of the Catalog and Its Integration with Other Discovery Tools* (Washington, DC: Library of Congress, 2006), www.loc.gov/catdir/calhoun-report-final.pdf.

4

The Portal Problem

The Twin Plights of the Encyclopaedia Britannica *and the Library Collection*

IN 2012, the *Encyclopaedia Britannica* announced its intention to cease publication in print and move entirely online. Immediately, the breast-beating and garment-rending began in the press. "Encyclopedia Britannica Goes Obsolete" moaned the Cleveland Plain Dealer.[1] "What Killed the Encyclopaedia Brittanica [*sic*]?," asked a blogger at the *Chicago Tribune*.[2] Over at *USA Today*'s *BookBuzz* blog, the cry was "RIP Britannica" ("the leather-bound classics are no more").[3] Of course, these writers all go on to explain that the *EB* itself isn't really dead, but the headlines shout a less-nuanced message that is reverberating everywhere, and it's a dramatic one: the *Encyclopaedia Britannica* as we know it—i.e., as a much-beloved, print-based monument to Western civilization—is no more.

To those who believe that the *Britannica* is dead because it's no longer publishing in print, I'd like to offer a small but significant correction: you're right that it's dead, but you're wrong about the reason. The *Britannica* isn't a victim of the obsolescence of print; it's a victim of the ineffectiveness of portals.

Let's dispense with the format issue quickly. I don't imagine I'll attract too many outraged comments by pointing out that the idea of publishing reference sources in print format is now fully ridiculous. Print is wonderful for extended linear reading, but it's a terrible platform for research and an even worse one for distribution. If you want

This essay was originally published in two parts—"Part 1: The Plight of the Britannica" and "Part 2: The Plight of the Library Collection"—in *The Scholarly Kitchen* (blog), March 22 and April 16, 2012.

to help people find discrete pieces of information, burying them in a large document that can be searched only by reading the whole thing (or by recourse to a crude index) is a terrible way to go about it. And if you want to distribute information to a large number of people, attaching it to a heavy physical object (let alone, in the case of the *Britannica*, thirty-two such objects) is no way to do it. The days of the printed encyclopedia are over, long over, and thank heaven for that.

But the obsolescence of print as a research medium is not what has killed the *Britannica*. The problem *Britannica* faces is the one faced by all information portals, regardless of format or platform: they tend to offer too much of the wrong kind of value, and too little of the right kind.

What value proposition does *Britannica* offer? We think of an encyclopedia as comprehensive—offering information on any topic you can think of. (Think about what we mean when we describe a source as "encyclopedic.") But, in reality, what an encyclopedia offers is the opposite of comprehensiveness. It offers a distillation or, more accurately, a selection: a superficially large-looking, but in reality tiny, collection of the information that is out there in the world. Even during the Gutenberg Era, the *Britannica*'s claim to cover "the breadth of human knowledge" was overblown; in the era of networked digital information, that claim borders on hilarious. To begin one's research with an encyclopedia is to start with a narrow and constricted strategy, not a broad one. This same problem applies to virtually any information portal.

People understand this instinctively, I think. That's why pitching one's portal to researchers by saying, "Start your search for chemistry information here!" or "We offer everything you need to know about copyright law!" isn't usually very effective—everyone knows that there's no such thing as a truly comprehensive, single source for information on chemistry or copyright law, or on virtually any other topic.

So if the *Britannica*'s offer of breadth is (like that of any encyclopedia) something of a mirage, then what does it offer that its competitors, such as *Wikipedia*, do not? Easy: authority. "Britannica provides you with the assurance that all information is authoritative and correct," the company tells us. And on the face of it, that sounds like a pretty solid value proposition. But here's the problem: lots of other online sources provide information that can reasonably be expected to be correct as well, and they don't charge you $69.95 a year (or $1,400 for the print, if you acted quickly) for access. Most of our information queries aren't terribly authority-sensitive—we often have little need of the assurance that the *Britannica* is selling. And when we do need really authoritative information, we're not likely to start our research in an encyclopedia.

Unless it's *Wikipedia*. Everyone criticizes *Wikipedia* because it's crowdsourced, and its authority is therefore suspect. But it offers something *Britannica* doesn't: a reasonable expectation of comprehensiveness, along with a reasonable expectation of correctness, at no charge.

Before committing myself publicly to that statement, I decided to give it a quick test. So I selected a topic that I know something about—clawhammer banjo playing—and looked it up in both sources. *Britannica* has no entry for "clawhammer banjo." So I looked up "banjo" instead and found a 250-word entry that touches exceedingly lightly on the physical design, origins, and uses of the instrument itself. Then I looked up "clawhammer banjo" in *Wikipedia*. There I found a 1,500-word entry that explains the mechanics of the playing style, lists significant artists and recordings, discusses clawhammer techniques as applied to instruments other than the banjo, and even dedicates a section to the all-important clawhammer-vs.-frailing controversy. Can I trust *Wikipedia*'s authority implicitly? Well, the fact that I see nothing in its "clawhammer banjo" entry that contradicts the things I know on the topic does tend to increase my confidence—not only in that entry, but in the others I'll encounter in *Wikipedia* down the road.

All of this is to say that *Britannica*'s challenge in the future is not going to be convincing people that it offers value. It's going to be convincing people that the particular value proposition it offers—a very small amount of highly reliable information—is worth paying for, given that people can easily get a very large amount of reasonably reliable information for free.

The challenge I have just described for the *Britannica* is also, incidentally, a major challenge facing libraries. The library collection is simply a bigger version of the encyclopedia: a seemingly exhaustive but actually (in the great majority of cases) very limited information portal that invites increasingly skeptical customers to "start your research here."

It's worth asking why a patron would (or should) want to start his or her research with the library collection. The answer will obviously depend on what kind of research is being done. If the patron is looking for a known item, then the question he is asking himself is, "Can I get quick and easy access to Document X?" The library does a good job of answering that question for its patrons. Library catalogs are generally pretty effective tools for known-item searching, and academic libraries have gotten quite good at providing easy access to the items in their collections, many now going so far as to offer free on-campus delivery of books and personal electronic delivery of articles.

But known-item searching constitutes only a small part of the scholarly research process. A much larger and arguably more important part of that process is the one that involves the question "Is there any such thing as a document dealing with Topic X?" The traditional library is, and always has been, poorly positioned to answer that question. While the library catalog can tell you whether or not it holds a book or an article on Topic X, it should be obvious that this question is more or less beside the point to a researcher, whose world is not defined by the boundaries of the library collection. Finding relevant documents or citations among the library's offerings doesn't answer the question fully (because there may be other such documents out there as well), and establishing a lack of them in the library doesn't answer the question at all.

There was a time—not very long ago—when the boundaries of one's local library collection did more or less define one's functional information world, and therefore the functional difference between these two questions ("Does my library own . . . ?" and "Is there such a thing as . . . ?") was much smaller. During that period, it made more sense to conflate those questions, and it made sense for libraries to encourage their patrons to "start your research here"—not that such encouragement was really necessary, as patrons had few other options. The fact that the library's collection was severely limited in coverage and that it was difficult to navigate, reachable only by travel, and open only part of the day posed little threat to the library's position as an information and research portal because it had no real competitors for that position.

Obviously, the information environment now teems with such competitors. But much more importantly, it's now very difficult for any new entrant to the portal marketplace to get a foothold. Those who want quick information on a particular topic and might once have turned to a traditional encyclopedia now have *Wikipedia*—which, again, is free, very easy to use, much more comprehensive in its coverage than any traditional encyclopedia, and reasonably authoritative. And those who want to figure out whether there is such a thing as a book or an article on Topic X now have Google—which is free, is very easy to use, and searches an astronomically huge (though not absolutely comprehensive) array of documents, many of which can be directly accessed in their entirety right from the search results, and others of which are discoverable as citations. Taken together, Google and *Wikipedia* arguably do an awful lot of what the library once did, and they do it more effectively, more conveniently, and for a much, much larger population than any individual library can serve. And they never close.

One obvious response to this argument is that part of the library's value lies in its selectiveness. Like an encyclopedia, it not only includes but also excludes. This means that the library's value proposition is not just that it includes everything you'll need, but also that you won't have to waste a lot of time slogging through what you don't need. The problem with this value proposition is that it constitutes a solution to a problem that many of us actually experience quite rarely these days: that of being overwhelmed by information. We don't actually have to slog through masses of irrelevant search results very often. Yes, results of a Google search might number in the millions. But its sorting algorithms have gotten so good at intuiting what the searcher is looking for that it's rarely necessary to look beyond the first page of results to find exactly what one is after. Even if you need a wider range of sources, you will often find as much as you need within the first few screens of the search results; the fact that the entirety of those results tails off into hundreds of thousands of other hits doesn't usually impinge on one's searching experience.

The simple fact (and a slightly terrifying one, if you're a professional discriminator) is that selectivity offers less value in an environment of networked online access and full-text searchability than it did when information was housed in printed documents. One purpose of selectivity is to keep the size of the document manageable—but if you don't have to carry the document on a bike or store it on a shelf and can search its entire text without recourse to an index, then document size becomes a much less relevant factor. Another goal of selectivity is to save the neophyte the effort of trying to figure out what's essential and what isn't. This is an honorable endeavor, but it assumes that people need access only to what we librarians consider essential (or even of high quality). In reality, researchers' needs vary widely from person to person and from project to project, and they may well need access to materials that we would not consider to be core, or even reliable, resources.

A more encouraging fact for libraries is that while both *Wikipedia* and Google offer unprecedented coverage and ease of access, neither of them offers a staff of dedicated helpers ready and waiting to help researchers shape their projects and locate relevant and high-quality sources. This is significant, and it represents one of the traditional library's stronger value propositions (although as a service model, it suffers from serious structural limitations).[4] As long as students and researchers believe that they need help, librarians will likely have an important role to play.

But in its fight to retain a strong position in the marketplace of researchers' time and attention, I think the library's most powerful weapon is the type of material we usually refer to as "special collections." Patrons can get commercially published books and articles from any number of sources, but if your library owns a truly unique document (like a daguerreotype portrait of a nineteenth-century actor, or the handwritten diary of a Mormon pioneer, or a typescript transcription of an oral history), then access to that document constitutes a genuinely unique value proposition. Historically, we in research libraries have tended to consign special collections to something of a ghetto—a benign and beloved one to be sure, but one that is somewhat outside the mainstream of everyday library services.

That has to change. Serving as a broker for resources that exist in many different copies in multiple formats and that can be found easily through Amazon or iTunes and purchased at reasonable prices is not an area of growing opportunity for libraries. Where we offer real and unique value, value that separates us from the competition, is in those areas in which we have no competition.

Is there enough demand for such resources to keep us in business? One problem with focusing on these materials is that (unlike our general collections) they're likely to be of serious interest to a relatively small subset of our local client base. One solution to this problem is, of course, digitization, by which we can make much (if not all) of the relevant content accessible to an audience of billions. So then the next question is this: Can we convince our sponsoring institutions that supporting the provision of that kind of value to billions of people who are mostly outside of our service remit is the best way to invest institutional funds?

NOTES

1. Regina Brett, "Encyclopedia Britannica Goes Obsolete . . . What's Next?," *The Plain Dealer*, March 18, 2012: A2, www.cleveland.com/brett/blog/index.ssf/2012/03/encyclopedia_goes_obsolete_wha.html.

2. Eric Zorn, "What Killed the Encyclopaedia Brittanica?," *Change of Subject* (blog), *Chicago Tribune*, March 19, 2012, http://blogs.chicagotribune.com/news_columnists_ezorn/2012/03/what-killed-the-encyclopedia-brittanica.html.

3. Lindsay Deutsch, "The Buzz in Books: RIP Britannica, New Cassandra Clare Series," *Book Buzz* (blog), *USA Today*, March 14, 2012, http://books.usatoday.com/bookbuzz/post/2012-03-14/the-buzz-in-books-rip-britannica-new-cassandra-clare-series/647874/1.

4. For further discussion of these limitations, see essay 15 in this volume.

5

On Necessity, Virtue, and Digging Holes with Hammers

HAVE YOU NOTICED that when people wear vests, they often leave the bottom button unfastened? There's apparently a historical explanation. I've been told that centuries ago there was a particularly overweight English king who, unable to fasten the bottom button on his waistcoat, decided that he would "make of necessity a virtue" and decreed that all of his subjects should henceforth leave the bottom waistcoat button undone as a matter of fashion.

I've never been able to verify that story, but whether or not it's true, it does illustrate a general human trait: our tendency to take behaviors or practices that are imposed on us by circumstance and eventually turn them (in our minds, anyway) into virtues.

There's not necessarily anything wrong with that tendency—kept within bounds, it can help us deal constructively with problems that can't be fixed. But sometimes things change, and the barriers that held us back in the past fall away. When that happens, we sometimes continue thinking and behaving as if the barriers still existed, and we may slide into an unhealthy veneration for behaviors that made sense when the barriers were there—adaptive behaviors can come to gain lives of their own as character-building "virtues."

In libraries, I think we need to reexamine some of what we've come to consider "virtuous" in our attitudes and behavior. Are these attributes and practices really virtues, or are they only ways of making necessary evils feel less onerous? And are they still necessary?

This essay was originally published as "Necessity, Virtue, and 'Research Skills'" in *Against the Grain* 19, no. 4 (September 2007): 76.

These thoughts came to mind during a discussion we were having in my library some time ago. Some of us were arguing about the importance of imparting research skills to students. My position was that we should focus more energy on making our resources easy to use and less energy on trying to make our patrons better users. Others felt that training students to be skillful and wise users of information resources is essential if we want to help them prepare for the future. One comment in particular made me stop and think. "Learning research skills," said one member of the library staff, "is one of the most important aspects of our students' education."

Why do we believe that? It certainly sounds reasonable—it may even sound like something close to a professional core value—and few of us would disagree with that sentiment in conversation. But why?

I think part of the answer lies in the ambiguity of the concept of "research skills." If we mean the ability to discriminate between relevant and irrelevant information, or between the authoritative and the merely assertive, or between reliable sources and unreliable ones, then we're clearly talking about an essential part of education. But if we mean the ability to locate resources (prior to judging their worth)—that is, the ability to actually find books or articles on a topic, to search accurately for resources within a database, or to locate copies of documents that have been cited by others—then I think we confuse necessity with virtue when we assert the importance of that skill.

I think our profession may have experienced a kind of collective psychic damage as the result of our centuries-old dependence on paper and ink as an information matrix. Fifteen years into the electronic revolution, we've almost forgotten how terribly difficult it was to locate information when our only finding tools were card catalogs and printed indexes. Let's make no mistake here: that period was not the good old days—it was the dark ages, a time when people were kept ignorant of vital information because it could be distributed to them only in a slow, wasteful, and expensive manner, and once distributed it could be used only at the cost of significant effort, and even then it couldn't be effectively searched. No one loves printed books more than I, but loving books should not mean being willfully blind to what they do well and what they do badly. What they are very good for is extended, linear reading; what they are exceptionally bad for is distributing information, and for finding particular pieces of information. Searching for information in a printed book is like using a hammer to dig a hole: it can be done, but only with a huge investment of wasted effort.

I suspect that the "core value" of patron education has arisen in our profession largely because we've come to confuse the necessity of print era research skills with the virtue of careful scholarship. For centuries, doing research has been a matter of digging a hole with a hammer. College was where most of us were trained in the proper use of hammers for digging, and many of us became quite good at it. Now we see the world around us (especially students) using those new-fangled shovels, and we're tempted to grumble about the hammer-wielding skills that no one bothers to acquire anymore. But why should we lament the passing of skills that were needed primarily to adapt to a bad situation that no longer obtains? Putting information online doesn't completely eliminate the necessity of searching, or of acquiring basic research skills—but it does give us the opportunity to make many of those skills obsolete.

Do we lose something when we make it possible for our patrons to get what they need with little or no effort? That's frankly a frivolous question, one with a simple and obvious answer but also the capacity to invoke almost limitless hand-wringing and time-wasting bloviation. The answer is, yes, of course we lose something. No change comes without loss. The important and constructive question is whether we are left with a net loss or with a net gain. Do our patrons get "spoiled" when we "spoon-feed" them the information they need? Maybe. But we should rejoice in spoiling our patrons in this way. The ability to make information easy to get is one in which we should revel and take pride. The less time our patrons have to spend in searching, the more time will be available to them for actual reading, and for thinking about what they read. Anyone who does not want people to spend less time searching and more time reading and thinking has, I suggest, no business in the library profession.

But there are other things that we do NOT lose, regardless of what some in our profession believe. Online access does not necessarily preclude browsing by subject, nor does it eliminate the element of serendipity from research. It's just as easy to come across an unanticipated discovery in database search results as on a bookshelf. There may be titles that would have been discovered on a physical shelf that would not be discovered in electronic search results, but the reverse is also true. And since a database contains far more information than any bookshelf could, the serendipity argument is really an argument in *favor* of more online searching, not against it—the likelihood of coming across unanticipated but good and relevant information sources in a database is far greater than the likelihood of doing so while browsing in a print collection.

Am I arguing that ease of access is the ultimate virtue in libraries? Not quite. Ease of access doesn't justify every conceivable expense, and of course there are online products that are necessary but notoriously difficult to use (our online catalogs perhaps chief among them). For now, it remains necessary to gain a certain level of skill in order to find the right information sources. But let's not confuse that necessity with virtue.

6

Can, Should, and Will

Part 1: Because What Libraries Need Is One More Venn Diagram

I came up with the diagram below (see figure 1) while I was thinking about library management during a lull in traffic at the reference desk recently. My original intent was sort of wryly humorous (it *is* hilarious, don't you think?), but the more time I spend looking at it, the more I think it's a potentially valuable tool for helping give shape to conversations about priority-setting and decision-making in libraries, and maybe in other organizations as well. Let's tease out a few of its implications.

First of all, some assumptions underlying the diagram are these:

1. We will not do anything that's impossible (that's why the "Will" circle is entirely contained by the "Can" circle).
2. There are things that we arguably should do that are not possible (which is why the "Can" circle is not entirely contained in the "Should" circle; more about this below).
3. Of the things we do, some will inevitably be the wrong things (as represented by the portion of the "Will" circle that falls outside the "Should" circle).

Now, it may seem strange that the circle defining what "should" be done is so big and that it overlaps only partially with the one defining what "can" be done. Does it really make sense to say there are things that *should* be done but *can't*?

This essay was originally published as two columns in *Library Journal*'s *Academic Newswire*, November 29, 2013, and January 16, 2014. Reprinted by permission.

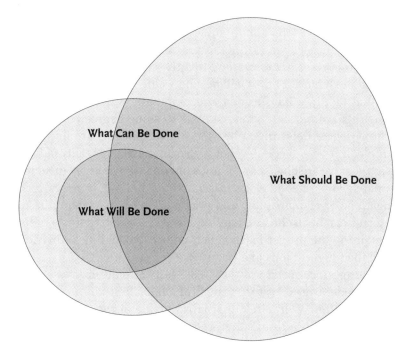

Figure 1

Yes, I think it does—and anyone who has spent time in library meetings will probably understand why. Sometimes we find ourselves spending meeting time on discussions of things it would be nice to do, but which are impossible. These discussions are usually prompted by someone who says something beginning with the words "If only we could . . ." The temptation to start down this topical road is intense because talking about "if only" can offer so much bittersweet pleasure. "If only we had another $500,000 in our materials budget"; "If only we could hire one more full-time staff person to work on the institutional repository"; "If only the faculty cared more about open access"; etc. Since there's a functionally unlimited number of things we arguably "should" do, and since we can actually do a relatively small number of those things, the "Should" circle is larger than the "Can" circle and the two overlap only partially.

Now to be clear, I'm not saying that we should simply sit back and be content with our current options and capabilities; on the contrary, we need to be constantly working to enlarge the borders of the "Can" circle. Doing so is often possible if we're intrepid and resourceful, and if we give our staff room and permission to try things out, innovate, and make mistakes. So talking in terms of "if only" is not necessarily a waste of time—it can lead us in practically fruitful directions. But it's also important not to pretend that the circle of "Can" is infinitely expandable. It isn't, it never will be, and we need to make sure we deal with that fact in a hardheaded and pragmatic way even as we seek to push its boundaries. This reality is to some degree concrete and to some degree determined by mission. All budgets are limited, for example. But on a deeper level, it is also an inevitable reality of librarianship that we are always spending someone else's money in support, ultimately, of someone else's mission, and that fact imposes certain obligations of responsibility and pragmatism on us. Talking in blue-sky terms can be useful and fruitful, but it can also be a waste of time. Maintaining the proper balance between responsibility and vision is one of the toughest jobs of a library leader.

The imperfect overlap of the "Will" and "Should" circles is where library leaders need to focus most of their attention and concern. The part of the "Will" circle that falls outside of the "Should" circle represents all those things that we do in the library even though we shouldn't. Clearly, our goal when making decisions and taking action should be to move the "Will" circle as fully into the "Should" circle as possible, though I think it's extremely unlikely (bordering on impossible) for any organization to make them overlap perfectly. No matter how hard we try, we will almost certainly end up doing some things we shouldn't. When that happens accidentally and despite our best efforts, it's a problem; when we (or members of our organization) do it more or less intentionally—either out of philosophical opposition or willful negligence—it's a much bigger problem. In any case, the verb tense here is significant: certain things *will* always get done; inevitably, some subset of those things *will* be the right thing. We want that subset to be as large as possible. And, of course, the "Will" circle itself is going to be bigger at some libraries, and at certain times, and smaller at others; sometimes we get more done and sometimes less. But it's inevitable that it will never fall entirely inside of the "Should" circle.

Those readers who are paying close attention may be experiencing a nagging sensation in the back of the brain. That nagging sensation is saying, "This whole conversation assumes a coherent understanding of what separates that which *is* from that which *should be*." That is indeed a big assumption, and this brings us to the issue of science versus religion.

Part 2: Science and Religion in the Library

Let me start out by acknowledging that "Science and Religion in the Library" is a provocative phrase, and to some degree, it's meant to be. Let me explain what I mean by it.

For my purposes here, I'm going to define as "science" those aspects of library work that deal with *figuring out and describing things as they are* and as "religion" those that deal with *figuring out how things should be and why they should be that way.* In the sense that I'm using the terms here, science is descriptive and religion is prescriptive; science is involved with "is" questions, while religion is involved with "should" questions. Both are important: On the "science" side, we need to know whether and to what extent our resources are being used by patrons, how much money is left in the budget, and where current trends will take us if they continue. On the "religion" side, we need to be clear on the ultimate goals behind what we do and on the values that inform our policies and practices. Furthermore, unless there's considerable agreement between library leaders and staff as to those foundational values, we are liable to find ourselves working at cross-purposes with one another.

The Venn diagram offered above illustrates three spheres of endeavor in the library, two of which represent the things we *should* do (which is a "should," or religious, question) and those we *can* do (which is an "is," or science, question). Both kinds of questions are very important, and recognizing the difference between them is equally so.

In the library, we are constantly faced with "science" questions. For example:

"How often do our patrons use *Chemical Abstracts*?"
"At what point in the future will we have to start canceling individual journal subscriptions in order to continue paying for our comprehensive Elsevier journal package?"
"What has been the ten-year trend line for book circulation in our library?"
"Is the information in this catalog record accurate?"

I characterize these as "science" questions because they deal with data that can be detected, analyzed, and measured, and from which inferences and projections can be made. Different people may disagree about the answers, but at least in principle the disagreements can generally be settled by an appeal to objective facts and data. The answers to these questions will tell us what *is*, but they will not, in and of themselves, tell us what we *should do*. In order to proceed from seeing what *is* to deciding what *ought to be*, we will have to bring a very different set of questions into play. These might include the following (notice the "should" terms in italics):

"Are our patrons using *Chemical Abstracts* at a level that *justifies* the expense?"

"Which individual journal subscriptions *should* we cancel before we start seriously considering unbundling the Big Deal?"

"Given the circulation trend line, would it be *wise* to redistribute our materials budget?"

"Do we have the *right amounts* of the *right information* in our catalog records?"

Each of the above is a "should" question rather than an "is" question. I categorize them as religious, not because they have to do with the supernatural, but because we won't be able to answer them by simply appealing to facts; in order to answer them, we will have to appeal to values. And this is where things can get dicey in the library. When two people disagree about whether *Chemical Abstracts* got 100 uses or 1,000 uses in the previous month, the dispute can be settled by an appeal to data; but when they disagree about whether the usage is sufficient to justify renewal, a different dimension of decision-making comes into play. "Sufficiency to justify" is not an "is" criterion, but a "should" criterion, and can be answered only by reference to values.

Most of us understand this more or less intuitively. If a colleague says, "I reject your circulation data because they say that our patrons decreasingly value the book collection," most of us will recognize that this stance represents an inappropriate conflation of "is" and "should" ("I reject your data because I wish they reflected a different reality"). But we aren't always as strictly clear about this important distinction in our meetings and policy discussions as we should be. Too often, we do conflate "is" and "should" considerations in ways that make it harder to solve problems and serve our patrons. It's understandable, of course. Consider how similar they can be, at least on the surface:

IS: "We can't afford to give our patrons everything they want."

SHOULD: "It's not our job to give patrons everything they want."

IS: "We have to cut *Journal X* if we're going to subscribe to *Journal Y*."
SHOULD: "*Journal Y* is too expensive and its publisher makes too much money."

IS: "We are regularly losing staff who leave for higher-paying jobs."
SHOULD: "We don't pay our staff enough."

Sometimes it's even harder to tell the difference between "should" and "is" statements because one is couched in the terminology of the other; the phrase "We can't do that" might mean "We don't have sufficient resources to do that," or it might mean "Doing that would constitute a breach of our values and mission." The same is true of statements like "We can't afford *Journal X*" (which usually means "Subscribing to *Journal X* would require us to cancel something more important") and "We can't hire so-and-so" (which may mean either "He doesn't meet the posted minimum requirements" or "I think he's an unacceptable candidate").

Again, it's important to emphasize that "science" questions are not better or more important than "religion" questions, nor vice versa. Both are essential. But if we're going to manage our resources and serve our patrons well, then recognizing and dealing with the differences between those kinds of questions is also essential. What does recognizing and dealing with them mean? In practice, for the most part, it means simply paying attention and guiding discussion (especially in meetings) accordingly. If you're running a meeting and encounter religious statements masquerading as science, it might be a good idea to gently unmask them: "John, you mentioned that we can't afford *Journal X*. It looks to me like we could afford it if we canceled these three titles from our annual review list. Is it possible that would be a good trade-off?" Do make sure you unmask them gently, though. No one likes having their religion challenged, no matter what it is.

7

How Sacred Are Our Patrons' Privacy Rights? Answer Carefully

IN 2014, the always-difficult issue of patron privacy arose again in the wake of revelations about problems with a version of Adobe Digital Editions (ADE)—specifically, the fact that version 4 of that e-reader software gathered highly specific data about individual users' reading behavior and transmitted it, unencrypted and with all identifying information included as well as other data culled from users' machines, back to Adobe.

Understandably and rightly, the fact that this was happening ignited something of a firestorm in the library world and elsewhere. Also understandably and also rightly, it led to hand-wringing and soul-searching within the library profession, as well as some intramural vituperation, particularly from those who had never been comfortable with the information ecology's marked drift in a digital and networked direction over the previous couple of decades.

For what it's worth, I would like to provide another perspective on this issue and its implications for library services, one based on two interlocking propositions.

Proposition #1: Our Patrons' Privacy Is Not Ours to Mess With

This proposition is pretty uncontroversial, I think, and it means that when we're entrusted with information about our patrons and their use of library resources and services, we have to be absolutely scrupulous about safeguarding it for as long as it's retained. In fact, I'll go fur-

This essay was originally published in *Library Journal*'s *Academic Newswire*, October 23, 2014. Reprinted by permission.

ther and say that more than just being uncontroversial, the truth of this proposition is actually trivially obvious.

However, the obvious and easily acceptable proposition that our patrons' privacy is not ours to mess with addresses only one dimension of the patron privacy issue: the fact that we have no right to breach patrons' privacy ourselves. It also raises a more complex and difficult question: To what degree will we leave privacy decisions in the hands of our patrons themselves, and to what degree will we take those decisions out of their hands? In other words, this is the access-vs.-privacy question, and it's difficult because it forces us to choose between several fundamental library values. Or, more accurately in this case, it forces us to grapple with two different (and to some degree conflicting) expressions of a single fundamental library value, which is the freedom to read. We express that value, on the one hand, by giving our patrons access to books and letting them read whatever they want, without restriction; we also express it, on the other hand, by ensuring to the best of our ability that they will be able to read whatever they wish without being surveilled. So what do we do when we can't give them access to what they want to read in a way that completely prevents surveillance?

For the moment, let's set aside the important question of whether things can be fixed so that the choice between access and privacy is obviated. Fixing the system may well be possible in the future, and librarians are uniquely well positioned to be major contributors to the process of making that happen. But, for the sake of argument, let's assume that for right now we do have to make that choice for at least some of the books that our patrons want to read, and that we'll keep having to make that choice for some time to come. If this is the reality, then for now we really do have to choose, to some degree, between providing access and protecting privacy. Let's look at some of the issues that bear on that choice, and let's start by looking at the second of the two interlocking propositions I alluded to earlier.

Proposition #2: Our Patrons' Privacy Is Theirs to Mess With

The fact that our patrons' privacy isn't ours to mess with begs the question: Whose is it? And the answer, I believe, is that our patrons' privacy is theirs to mess with. Taking that reality seriously means that just as we need to treat as sacrosanct the confidentiality of patron data that we hold, we also have to treat as sacrosanct our patrons' right to make decisions about their own privacy.

To say that this right is sacrosanct isn't to say that our patrons can be counted on always to make wise privacy decisions. It's only to say that we shouldn't take upon ourselves the role of decider when it comes to other people's privacy any more than we should do so when it comes to other people's decisions about reading; we don't tell them what to read, we don't tell them what to think, we don't tell them how to use the information we provide them, and I certainly don't see how we can decide for them what constitutes an acceptable or unacceptable use of their private information.

What does this mean in real life? In the case of the ADE issue, for example, let's suppose that my library is offering e-books that are available on only that platform and that, for the moment, there is no way to fix the problem of ADE sending personal information about readers and their behavior to its parent company. In that situation, if my library is providing those books, then I don't believe I have the right simply to continue with business as usual, giving my patrons access to e-books in that way and disregarding their privacy rights. So in the absence of a short-term fix to the problem itself, it seems to me that I have two options: either stop providing access to those e-books or inform my patrons of what's happening and let them decide for themselves whether access to those books is worth the loss of privacy that using them entails.

Values in Conflict

Neither of these options is a comfortable one, because each of them simultaneously supports and conflicts with my patrons' freedom to read.

The first option supports the basic library value of freedom to read by ensuring that patrons' reading behavior won't be monitored by third parties. The problem, of course, is that it ensures that privacy by making the books inaccessible. That strikes me as problematic—kind of like preventing burglary by burning your house down. (Simply providing the same books in print format will in many cases be impossible because my library could never afford to provide access to as many print books as it can e-books.)

But the second option, informing patrons about the privacy issue and letting them choose for themselves to read under surveillance, is also problematic because it assumes that my patrons will (a) pay attention to the notifications we put in place about the risks inherent in using these e-books and then will (b) make good privacy decisions based on that information. As we all know, people are by no means always good judges of what's in their best interests and they don't always pay attention to urgently relevant information or make good decisions based on it.

So what do we do?

What Do We Mean When We Say "Privacy Is Sacred"?

As one approach to untangling this problem, consider this: We librarians recently observed Banned Books Week, during which we celebrated "the freedom to seek and to express ideas, even those some consider unorthodox or unpopular"—or, in other words, our determination not to let other people tell our patrons what they can do with their minds. Surely this isn't because we believe all books are equally worthy of our patrons' attention, or even that books are only capable of doing good in the world. If we believe that ideas are powerful, then we have to acknowledge that the power of ideas can be destructive as well as constructive—and yet our stance, as a profession, is (and I believe has to be) that we are going to let our patrons select for themselves the ideas they will invite into their minds. In other words, we know that some of our patrons' reading decisions will be bad—some of them will seek out, absorb, and eventually subscribe to ideas and principles that might lead them down paths that are destructive both to themselves and to others—but, nevertheless, we see the freedom to choose what one reads as too sacred to take away from them.

So here's the question for us in regard to e-books and patron privacy: How sacred is our patrons' right to privacy? Is it so sacred that only we, the library profession, can be entrusted with its care, since we very often have a better understanding of the implications of privacy decisions and can always be counted on to have the best interests of our patrons at heart? Or is it so sacred that we would never consider arrogating to ourselves the right to make our patrons' privacy decisions for them?

Now would be a very good time for each of us to decide where we stand on this question. And no matter which stance we choose, we'd better be ready to defend it—because either one is going to make some people angry.

8

Crazy Idea #274: Just Stop Collecting

FOR AS LONG as there have been libraries, the words "library" and "collection" have been almost interchangeable. The library was the books, or at least the building with the books in it, and without the books, it wouldn't have been a library. That's been the case since the earliest libraries were established. Our approaches to patron service and collection management have changed, but what has not changed is the centrality of a permanent collection, gathered and shaped in anticipation of users' needs, to the very idea of the library itself.

For centuries, this made perfect sense because our information access problems were shaped by three fundamental truths:

As individuals, we all needed more information than we could afford. No one had enough money to buy copies of all the information resources he'd ever need, or to store them even if he could. So we all got together as communities, pooled our money, and bought single copies of documents that members of the community could take turns using. The upside of this arrangement was that everyone in the community had more or less equal access to a relatively rich collection; the downsides were, first, that the collection was inevitably incomplete (no library met every patron's every possible need) and, second, that the collection was stored centrally, which meant that the user had to come to the collection—an arrangement that posed a minor inconvenience to some and made access impossible for others.

Information was slow and expensive to distribute. Another reason for building and maintaining a permanent collection was the slowness and expense of moving printed documents from one place to another. If a patron made a trip to the library to find a book and the book wasn't

---

This essay was originally published in *Against the Grain* 18, no. 4 (September 2006): 50–52.

there, the library could usually get a copy for her—eventually. But the process was clumsy and slow and expensive and required the patron to make a return trip to the library at some point in the future, assuming that the book would still be of use to her by that point. Thus, it made sense for a library to build as comprehensive a collection as it reasonably could, in anticipation of its patrons' needs. Of course, we couldn't anticipate patrons' needs perfectly, which meant that we ended up buying resources that no one wanted and failing to buy resources that they did want.

Relevant information was hard to find. Think back, if you can, to life before the World Wide Web. If you were contemplating a move to Des Moines and wanted to know how many days of sunshine that city has in an average year, or if you wanted to know when the salmon usually run in Kachemak Bay, then you had to make a trip to the library. One important reason for a library collection was to answer these kinds of questions—simple ones, but ones that relied on access to obscure and often costly sources.

In short, throughout human history, information has been expensive, unwieldy, and obscure. This was partly because information was expensive to create, but also because it was stored and transmitted in printed media (except, of course, in those cultures where it was stored mentally and transmitted orally, rendering it even more expensive and obscure, if quite a bit more portable). Storing print requires much labor and the investment of significant resources; once printed, the information is difficult, slow, and expensive to transport and can be searched only—if at all—by means of crude indexes, which themselves are very costly to create and which, by their nature, never fully index the texts to which they refer. For centuries, the library offered the best available solution to these problems.

The problem for libraries is that we no longer live in an information world that is fundamentally characterized by expense, unwieldiness, and obscurity. While it remains true that some information is expensive and hard to find, and much of it is still trapped in print formats and therefore difficult to distribute, *most of the information that most people need most of the time* is now available in electronic formats. Furthermore, a large and growing percentage of that information is freely available to the public, and zeroing in on the particular nugget of information one needs is easy and getting easier every day. In 2006, just about any ready-reference question could be better (i.e., more quickly, easily, and accurately) answered by recourse to the Internet than to a printed book. With online information, the problem of unwieldiness is solved because physical distribution is no longer necessary. The obscurity problem is largely (if not completely) solved by full-text searchability. The expense problem will always exist, though it's now mainly a problem for those with deep and complex research needs. Those in need of quick answers to general questions—who formerly had to make the same trip to the library that serious researchers had to make—can now find those answers in seconds without leaving their homes.

All of this raises a serious question for libraries. If the purpose of a permanent collection is to solve problems that have now largely been solved by forces outside the library, does it still make sense for us to build and maintain permanent collections? Forgive me as I lapse into business jargon, but why does it make sense to invest (wastefully and at great expense) in a "just-in-case" service model when a "just-in-time" alternative is available?

This, of course, begs a question: Is a "just-in-time" model really available to libraries? Do we really have the option of abandoning the idea of a permanent collection altogether and instead becoming a real-time, by-the-drink operation that responds immediately and effectively to patrons' expressed needs?

The answer is no. Not yet. For one thing, we don't want our patrons to have to talk to a librarian in order to get what they want. One of the beautiful things about a modern library is that you can browse around in it to your heart's content—we don't want to go back to the service counter mode of librarianship, one that requires patrons to supplicate the library staff in order to get what they need. For another thing, our budgets are limited and patrons' desires are potentially unlimited. If we don't ration our materials budgets but leave them at the real-time mercy of the demanding hordes, the money will disappear before everyone's needs have been met. One virtue of traditional collection development is that it distributes the materials budget in a rational way.

But what if we started moving in that direction? What if we shrank our idea of the collection until it resembled only a hard core of essential titles, titles that we have good reason to believe will get significant use, and thus freed up more of the materials budget to respond to real needs in real time? This would reduce the amount of money we waste on materials no one wants and increase the amount we spend on materials that are actually needed. Not every library could do this in equal degrees, of course; there are some libraries, like Harvard's, or the New York Public Library, that have missions (and budgets) specifically oriented toward creating and preserving comprehensive, permanent collections. Such collections are not just practical resources for the everyday user, but also monuments to Western civilization, and those collections serve an important purpose in society.

But they are also very much exceptions to the rule. Most libraries, whether public or academic or corporate or "special," have missions that are much more narrowly targeted, with budgets and physical space to match. For the average library to attempt to collect comprehensively and permanently on a "just-in-case" basis made much less sense in 2006 than it did in 1956—or even in 1990, before it was clear that the World Wide Web was about to turn the information economy upside down.

Almost all libraries now struggle to house and manage the collections they already have; at the same time, budgets are stagnant, serials inflation flirts with double digits, and new and expensive titles continue to proliferate. The implication seems obvious: when you're out of room and you're out of money, you're going to have to start buying less. Instead of figuring out how to ratchet down the activity of our current acquisition model, perhaps the time has come to move toward a different model altogether. It may well be that the very idea of a comprehensive and permanent library collection has outlived its usefulness.

9

Local and Global, Now and Forever

A Matrix Model of "Depth Perception" in Library Work

ACADEMIC LIBRARIES are in an interesting and difficult position, one that makes us different from most other public and private institutions. We are charged with meeting the immediate needs of students and faculty (needs that can usually be identified and defined with at least some degree of precision), but also with creating lasting collections that will meet the largely unpredictable needs of future users. At the same time, we also function as supportive infrastructure on our campuses, active contributors to the scholarly and creative output of our institutions and profession, and participants in a global scholarly communication ecosystem. Our functions are local and global, short-term and long-term, just-in-time and just-in-case.

Depth Perception: Spatial and Temporal

Working within this complex structure of needs and expectations requires us constantly to be shifting focus. Think about how your eyes work: they have muscles that contract and relax in order to adjust the distance between the retina and the lens, making it possible for you to shift your attention from objects that are far away to objects that are in the near distance and to objects that are very close. Depth perception is the ability to locate objects in space when they're at different distances from you.

Now consider how you think about the work you do in your library, whether it be as a support staffer, a librarian, a manager, or

This essay was originally published in *Against the Grain* 26, no. 5 (November 2014): 78–79.

an administrator. Is your focus generally on more distant and global issues (the scholarly communication system, copyright law, intellectual freedom), or on issues somewhere in the midrange (how the library's services support the institutional mission, whether your collection matches the curriculum, how your ILL operation works with those of other institutions in the state), or on issues that are very close and granular (whether your signage is helpful, how equipment is maintained, how budgets are managed)? I'll call this set of concerns the "spatial" vector of perspective.

The issue of perspective applies in a temporal sense as well as a spatial one. To pick a global issue (the scholarly communication system) as an illustration: Is your day-to-day focus mainly on long-term issues (Is the journal subscription model sustainable?), on midterm issues (What will be the state of the scholarly monograph five years from now?), or on short-term ones (What will happen if Journal X is bought by Publisher Y?)? I'll call this the "temporal" vector of perspective.

The interaction of these two vectors can be expressed simply in a two-dimensional matrix like the one below (see figure 1).

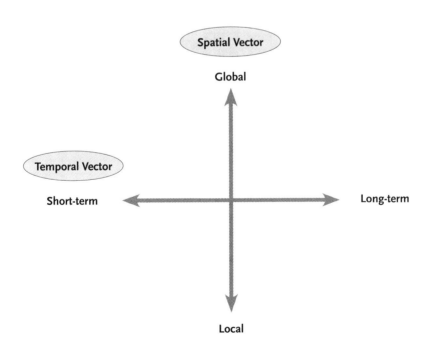

Figure 1

The general orientation of any particular librarian on any particular issue will fall somewhere in (or, more likely, across) the four quadrants defined by this matrix. So will the mission of an individual academic library—the library at a national university may be expected to focus substantially on its role as a long-term and comprehensive archive, while the library at a regional community college may be charged almost exclusively with serving students and faculty in the here-and-now. Most academic libraries serve some combination of these functions, but the mix will vary quite a bit from library to library, depending on the needs and missions of the institutions that host (and pay for) them.

Attitudes and Orientations

To help us think about the interactions and implications of these dynamics, I'll characterize each of the four quadrants with a phrase that seems to me to describe the overriding attitude that is predominant in each one—bearing in mind (and accepting, for the purposes of this model) that in each case, that phrase represents an oversimplification (see figure 2).

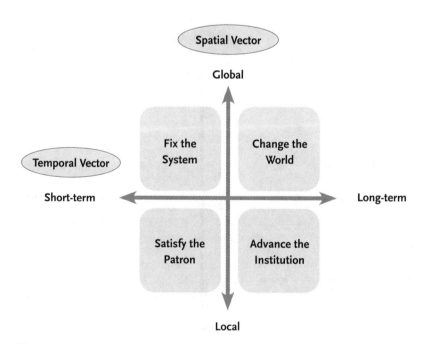

Figure 2

So, for example, if I think about a library policy or practice exclusively as it affects *my library's patrons* (local) in the *here and now* (short-term), my perspective on that policy or practice is falling squarely into the lower-left quadrant of this model ("Satisfy the Patron"). If I tend to focus on how it might affect the *world of scholarship* (global) in the *long run* (long-term), then my perspective on that issue falls into the upper-right quadrant ("Change the World"). And so forth.

Applying the Model

It's important to bear in mind that no quadrant in this matrix has a monopoly on right answers to the difficult questions facing us in libraries and the scholarly communication system. Each perspective has something to recommend it, and each poses potential problems. At every point in this model there is a mix of upsides and downsides, and this suggests that it would probably not be wise for any individual to pick a single spot in this matrix and plant a permanent ideological flag there.

For example, on the temporal vector: One upside of maintaining a long-term focus is that you may see threats coming on the horizon that those with a shorter focus do not. (For example, subscribing to comprehensive journal packages may provide spectacular value to patrons in the near term but may not be sustainable in the long run.) But a downside of the long-term perspective is that if you're not careful, you can let yourself be paralyzed by "what-ifs." The farther you look down the road, the more possible scenarios—many of them undesirable—you will see, and worrying too much about the risk of undesirable scenarios can lead you to miss out on important needs and opportunities in the near term. At the other end of the temporal spectrum, an upside of the short-term focus is that it makes you less easily distracted by "what-ifs" and more willing to try new things and take risks. But a downside of the short-term perspective is that it can lead to a posture of reactivity and a neglect of essential planning and strategy.

On the spatial vector: One upside of maintaining a global perspective is that it helps you to put your library work in a larger context and to see implications of your work that are not locally obvious. A downside of that perspective is that it can cause you to overlook the needs of your patrons and your local curriculum. At the other end of the spatial spectrum, an upside of the local focus is that it tends to attract more institutional support for the library, since it leads the library to position itself as a strategic partner on campus. A downside is that it may lead you to make decisions that contribute to global and systemic problems that go against the interests of students and scholars both locally and in the larger system.

Limiting Factors and Institution Mission

Now, the fact that no single quadrant in this model has a monopoly on "right" perspectives doesn't mean that no single perspective on any issue (or in any situation) can be called "right." And this brings up a very important caveat: While the range of personal and professional perspectives among us is likely to be very broad—some of us naturally tending to focus more on the global long-term, others on the local short-term, etc.—what varies much less is the variety of organizations that employ us. Each of us is employed by an organization that has an institutional focus that may or may not accord with our personal predilections, but that nevertheless *has to inform the focus of the work we do in the library.* This is actually true whether we work for libraries, publishers, foundations, grant makers, hospitals, government agencies, or any other organization. As professionals, we have an obligation to do more than just express our own attitudes and beliefs at work; while those attitudes and beliefs certainly will and should *inform* our work, they should *define* our work only to the degree that they match those of the institutions that employ us. If there is unsustainable friction between our own attitudes and our institutions' needs, then the professional and ethical thing to do is not to undermine the institution or ignore its mission, but—to be brutally frank—to look for other work.

Does this mean that we should do nothing to shift our institutions' values if we disagree or see problems with them? Absolutely not. All of us can be a force for positive change (as we understand it) within the institutions that employ us, and in fact I would argue that we have a moral—as well as professional—obligation to do so. We also usually have the opportunity to contribute to the shaping of institutional objectives and strategies, and we should actively pursue those opportunities. We will (and should) naturally bring our own perspectives and attitudes with us when we participate in shaping the future directions of our institutions.

But, ultimately, the institution is going to be what the institution is going to be. Sometimes our individual values and preferences will start to diverge from those of our institutions until there comes a point at which we have to decide whether or not we can continue to work for that institution.

What this implies, I believe, is that each of us needs to examine our own predilections and perspectives to see how they fall along the two dimensions defined by this matrix and then examine the institutional orientation that is defined by our campuses' and libraries' goals and strategies. Each of us should then ask herself or himself, "How close is the fit between what I want to do, what I believe is right, and my institution's mission and goals?" And if there's a lot of daylight between those two orientations, then the next—and much more difficult—question is, "What am I going to do about that?" The answer to that question will vary from person to person and from place to place, of course. For each of us, knowing where we stand on these important issues of depth perception will help us decide whether the place we are is the right one for us.

10

A Quiet Culture War in Research Libraries—and What It Means for Librarians, Researchers, and Publishers

I WOULD LIKE to begin by giving away the ending. The culture war that I believe is currently brewing in research libraries is between two general schools of thought: the first sees the research library's most fundamental and important mission as serving the scholarly needs of its institution's students, scholars, and researchers; the second sees the research library's most fundamental and important mission as changing the world of scholarly communication for the better.

It is important to bear in mind that these two endeavors are not mutually exclusive; on the contrary, they are not even in conflict with each other in principle. In practice, however, conflict between them is inevitable because the programs and projects they represent are in competition for the same pool of strictly limited resources—and that conflict is already in evidence both within and between our institutions.

Now, having given away the ending, I would like to back up and start at the beginning. I will do so with what I realize may sound like a rather odd statement: I believe that the conflict within libraries to which my title refers is rooted primarily in the various disruptions that have been caused by the information ecology's nearly wholesale move out of the print and into the online realm. The conflict arises not from the greater complexity of our new information environment, or from the greater pressure being put on our strictly limited resources, or from the changing expectations of our students, faculty, and researchers but, rather, from the fact that where once we had no choice but to focus primar-

---

This essay was originally published in *Insights* 28, no. 2 (July 2015).

ily on the local and immediate needs of that constituency, we are now faced with very difficult choices about where our primary focus should be, and the very fact that this variety of choices is now available to us is what gives rise to the conflict.

The Multidimensional Complexities of the Shift from Print to Online

When the scholarly information world moved dramatically out of the realm of physical objects and into that of a digital network, it made possible changes in perspective and function that have been quite dramatic for research libraries. These include:

A shift from object-gathering to access brokerage. The primary function of the library up until the mid-1990s was to gather, curate, and preserve physical objects onto which information had been printed. During this period, we were far less likely than we are now to question the viability or justice of the distribution system—it was what it was and we did the best we could with it. Since 1995, our function has been, increasingly, to secure for our patrons the collective right to access and use digital documents that are housed and cared for elsewhere. In this context, with many more access options available, it is easier (and more fruitful) to ask difficult questions about the justice and equity of the existing system.

A shift from institutional to global. Access to a printed book or journal issue is not scalable; no more than one or two people can use any physical document at any one time. Access to an e-book or e-journal, however, is (in functional terms) almost infinitely scalable. For this reason, libraries have recently found themselves able, for the first time in their history, to think in terms of providing access to constituencies far beyond the borders of their host institutions—a fact that sets us up for very difficult discussions about the appropriate use of local institutional resources.

A shift from simple issues to complex ones. When information was tied to physical objects, most of the issues we had to deal with when acquiring those objects were relatively simple—not necessarily easy, but relatively simple compared to the issues we deal with in an information environment characterized by licensed access to externally hosted content provided within the context of rights management systems.

A shift from toll access to open access. All of the shifts discussed above are, of course, what have made possible the emergence of an access system (or, more accurately, a complex of systems, models, and platforms) that makes both access to and unlimited reuse of scholarly information freely available to all who have access to the digital network.

These issues can, I believe, be boiled down to the following general categories of divisive issues at play in our environment:

- access
- cost
- rights
- funding

In our new information environment these issues are, first of all, no longer as clear-cut as before; second, each of our libraries is now in a position (technologically, at least) to address them on a global stage as well as a local one; third, our budgets are, in most cases, shrinking rather than growing. At the same time, we see demand for some of what we used to consider core functions of librarianship dropping and, in some cases, dropping precipitously. This situation creates ambiguity, which of course leads to fear, which in turn leads to conflict—though it is important to acknowledge that not all of the conflict I will describe arises from fear. Much of it arises from deep and genuine philosophical disagreement and from various parties in the system being deeply invested in mutually exclusive goals.

Local Responsibilities vs. Global Responsibilities

In this context of increasing complexity, expanding opportunities, and constricting resources, the big question that I believe is becoming increasingly fraught in our research libraries is this one: How should each of our libraries balance its responsibility to the needs of its host institution with its responsibility to do good and effect change in the larger world?

Again, we do not have to choose entirely between these two orientations; however, we do have to acknowledge that they are in tension with each other, for the simple reason that our resources are strictly limited and that every hour of time or dollar of budget allocation we spend on one thing is an hour or dollar that we cannot spend on something else.

The conflict that arises from this simple economic reality plays out in different ways in different contexts. For example:

The "Big Deal." There is a strong argument to be made that every time a library enters into a Big Deal package arrangement with a large and powerful publisher, it contributes to the perpetuation of an unsustainable and broadly harmful system, one that ties up large chunks of libraries' budgets and supports the publication of low-quality, low-demand journals. On the other hand, it may also be true that for a particular library, the Big Deal (despite all of its manifold downsides) is the most cost-effective way to provide its patrons with access to the content they need in order to do their work.

Open-access (OA) program memberships. A growing number of OA programs are emerging that rely for their funding, in whole or in part, on paid library memberships. Very often these programs provide little, if any, direct, local, and concrete benefit to the member library or its patrons; instead, they offer a mechanism by which the library may actively support broader and more open access to scholarship for the general public. Libraries that join up are simultaneously making a difference in the larger world and redirecting local funds away from the satisfaction of immediate and local needs.

Article processing charge (APC) subventions. Many libraries are experimenting with setting aside funds to underwrite APCs on behalf of local scholars and scientists who wish to publish in gold OA venues that impose author-side charges. This approach amounts to a redirection of funds very similar to that represented by paying for membership in an OA program. Money that could have been used to make a large number of articles available to the limited local community is instead used to make a small number of articles available to the general public

OA mandates. Libraries that succeed at establishing local OA mandates, or that urge such mandates on the faculty in their institutions, are (to the degree that they succeed in establishing them) contributing to a greater openness of scholarship and enabling global access to that scholarship, while at the same time creating structures that reduce the amount of control local researchers and faculty have over the disposition of their own work.

Interlibrary loan vs. short-term loan. When a patron needs a book or an article that is not held by his or her library, it is often faster, cheaper, and more efficient to purchase short-term access to an online version of that article or book than to borrow a copy from another library. However, many librarians object to this practice on the grounds that it may undermine the library's traditional rights under fair use, fair dealing, or first sale doctrines. By spending more on the traditional interlibrary loan approach, the library supports a global program at the expense of supporting local needs.

Soldiers and Revolutionaries

The tension between local and global orientations that inevitably arises in an environment of strictly limited resources in turn gives rise, it seems to me, to two general categories of orientation among librarians. I call these the "soldier" and the "revolutionary" orientations.

The soldier can be thought of as generally operating under "marching orders," which he takes from his institution's mission and strategic goals, and tends to focus mainly on local needs, the impact of library services on current patrons, and the library's alignment with its institutional mission. Those with a predominantly soldier mind-set will tend to think of the library primarily as a service and support program for its host institution. In particular, those with a predominantly soldier orientation will tend to:

- define stakeholders locally in both space and time: the library's central responsibility is to those patrons who are here, now;
- see compromise as an essential part of getting things done;
- tend to focus on solving problems that are local, tangible, and immediate;
- see the library primarily as an agent of its sponsoring institution;
- focus on responding to patrons' demonstrated behavior and desires;
- be willing to enter into commercial partnerships if doing so will help to solve immediate local problems;
- be oriented toward concrete tasks and outputs; and
- always be looking at the fiscal "bottom line" and watching for opportunities to strengthen it.

The revolutionary mind-set thinks less in terms of marching orders than in terms of global vision. A librarian with a predominantly revolutionary mind-set will tend to think more about the library's effect on the global scholarly community, its potential role in solving global and systemic problems, and the long-term impact of its collections and services in that context.

The revolutionary will tend to think of the library less as a service than as a leader and educator on campus. In particular, those with a more revolutionary mind-set will tend to:

- define stakeholders universally in both space and time: the library is responsible not only to patrons here and now but also (and maybe more importantly) to knowledge-seekers *everywhere*, both *now* and *in the future*;
- often see compromise as a betrayal of fundamental values;
- tend to focus on issues that are *universal, abstract, and future-oriented*;

- see the library primarily as a contributor to the larger world of scholarship;
- focus on educating and changing the behavior of patrons and on giving them what they should want (rather than what they may want);
- see cooperation with commercial entities as fundamentally morally suspect;
- be oriented toward broad social change; and
- see discussion of the "bottom line" as an encroachment of commercial thinking into a realm where it does not belong.

As a potential tool to help us think about this dynamic, I have published elsewhere a discussion of what I call the issue of "depth perception" in libraries,[1] which I suggest can be measured along two dimensions: one is spatial (defining a spectrum from local to global) and the other is temporal (defining a spectrum from short-term to long-term). The two-dimensional model shown in figure 1 defines four quadrants of orientation.

Overlaying the "soldier" and "revolutionary" orientations on this matrix yields a model as shown in figure 2.

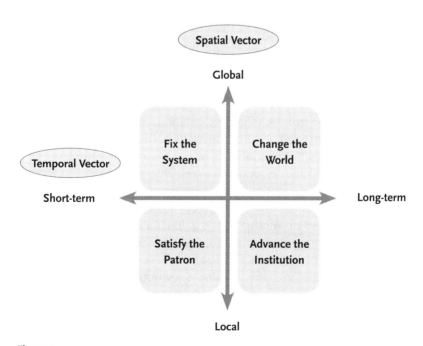

Figure 1

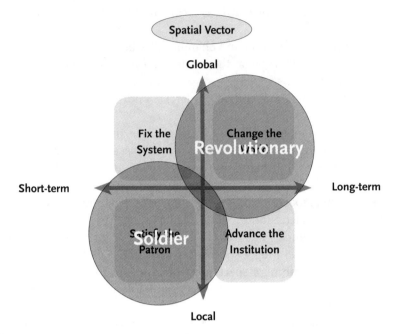

Figure 2

Three things about these categories should be clear:

- Hardly any individual librarian can be characterized as either a pure soldier or a pure revolutionary. This model is intended to characterize mind-sets and orientations, not individuals, and if it is useful at all, it will be to help us think about the balance of these two orientations in ourselves and our libraries (as expressed by policies and practices).
- Soldier and revolutionary orientations are spectrum values, not binary ones. One's mind-set is likely to lean more in one direction or another, but the likelihood of any individual librarian caring exclusively for the local patron or exclusively for the global system is very low.
- At any point on the soldier-to-revolutionary spectrum, a given position will present both strengths and weaknesses. Furthermore, a given position may be more or less "right" in context depending on the issue at hand.

What Do These Ideas Imply for Library Leadership?

Although there are relatively few librarians whose orientations can fairly be described as either exclusively that of the soldier or of the revolutionary, most of us lean in one direction or the other. Furthermore, every library's culture (as defined and created both by its leadership and by the totality of its employee orientations) will likely reflect an overall leaning in one direction or the other. To the degree that there is internal disagreement over what that orientation should be, there will be conflict within the library; to the degree that there is disagreement between the library and its sponsoring institution over what the library's orientation should be, there will be conflict between the library and its host.

How can such conflict be managed and dealt with? I propose the following stepwise approach:

- *Surface the issue.* Start with an assessment of the library's internal culture, by openly discussing the question of local vs. global orientation and bringing to the surface both the prevailing orientation within the library and any areas of significant disagreement that exist among library staff and/or between staff and leadership.
- *Resolve (or at least identify) internal inconsistencies.* The library should have a sense of where it generally stands, as an organization, on the spectrum of orientations between soldier and revolutionary. This stance may be expressed in a mission statement, a strategic plan, or (less effectively) as the sum total of the library's policies and practices.
- *Assess institutional alignment.* To what degree does the library's general orientation align with the mission and goals of the library's host institution?
- *Address disparities with campus administration.* To the degree that there is daylight between the library's orientation and the institution's mission and goals, this disparity should be discussed by the library director and the provost, vice president, or other administrator to whom he reports. The disparity may be of greater or lesser concern to the campus administration, but letting it continue without being addressed is both strategically unwise and, arguably, ethically questionable.
- *Consider opportunities to influence institutional mission and culture.* A disconnect between the library's orientation and that of its host institution does not always have to be resolved

by movement on the library's part. The library, as a centrally important component of the institution, has a role in helping to influence and define institutional directions. This is particularly true where librarians have faculty status. Where the library is in a position to influence the culture, mission, and goals of the larger institution, it should do so.

- *Where such influence is impossible or ineffective, realign the library.* This can be the most difficult step in the process. Ultimately, after the library and all other campus stakeholders have given their input and done their best to influence the institution's goals and orientation, final decisions will be made by those charged with determining those goals and that orientation. On most campuses, such decisions rest with some combination of the university president, vice presidents, chancellor, and board of trustees. If the final decision is to set the institution on a path that does not align well with the library's orientation, it is up to the library to reorient itself.

This brings us to the final, and perhaps most difficult, point I wish to make.

Soldiers Are Employees; Revolutionaries Are Freelance

It is a painful fact, but a fact nonetheless, that any library hosted by a larger institution—be it a university, a hospital, a research foundation, a corporation, or any other type of organization—does not have full independence of action and orientation. It is an organ of its host, and, I believe, it is ethically obligated to support the mission of its host. It is true that on many campuses, librarians have faculty status, and that faculty status confers upon those librarians a tremendous amount of independence of thought and action in their function as employees. Faculty members have great discretion within the scope of their positions: they have the right to define the content of their courses, to decide how they will teach, and to pursue their intellectual interests without constraint. However, just as the teaching faculty do not generally decide (as individuals) whether and how much they will teach, and just as the faculty (collectively) do not generally make the final decisions as to how many faculty the university will hire, or which programs will receive more or less funding, the library will not have the unilateral ability to determine its host institution's mission and strategic directions.

This fact has serious implications for the ultimate outcome of the culture war that I believe is currently brewing in the research library community. We are now working in an information environment that makes it possible for each library to exert a global influence in unprecedented ways. The desire to do so is both praiseworthy and solidly in keeping with many of what most of us would consider core values of librarianship. However, even as we experience varying levels of agreement among ourselves as to the proper distribution of our time and resources in pursuit of these two different orientations, virtually all of us continue to be supported entirely by funds that come from institutions that expect us to use those funds to support local needs and an institutionally defined mission. As long as it remains impossible to spend the same dollar twice, we will have no way to avoid choosing between programs that support local needs and those that support global ones, and as long as we depend on local resources to do so, we will have an ultimate obligation to act more like soldiers than like revolutionaries. Libraries that fail to do so will inevitably lose their institutional support—and with good reason.

NOTE

1. Rick Anderson, "Local and Global, Now and Forever: A Matrix Model of 'Depth Perception' in Library Work," *Against the Grain* 26, no. 5 (November 2014): 78–79. See also essay 9 in this volume.

11

Interrogating the American Library Association's "Core Values" Statement

OVER THE PAST couple of decades, we in libraries have been asking a lot of soul-searching questions about how we can best carry out our functions in a radically changed (and still-changing) information environment. This self-examination has led to many interesting conclusions and some pretty dramatic shifts in the ways libraries do business—almost always in the context of reaffirmations of the library's core mission and values. Less frequently have we asked ourselves whether the core principles that underlie traditional library service remain relevant and essential in and of themselves.

With that in mind, I decided to take a hard look at the "Core Values of Librarianship" statement at the American Library Association's website.[1] When I did so, I noticed two things.

First, as core values go, everything on the list looked pretty timeless to me; none of the values enumerated there seemed to me at risk of being obviated by structural changes in the information environment.

Second, however, I was struck by something else: the impression that the list has other problems not related to relevance or timeliness. In trying to understand and sort out those problems, I found myself dividing the list of values into three categories: those that strike me as representing fundamental principles, those that represent subordinate principles, and those that (bear with me, now) we might do well to question as core values of librarianship at all.

Let me try to explain what I mean.

This essay was originally published in *Library Journal*'s *Academic Newswire*, January 31, 2013. Reprinted by permission.

Fundamental Principles

Values that represent fundamental principles, it seems to me, are those that engage with the question "What are the deepest and most basic purposes of the library?" I suggest that of the values listed by the ALA as "core," those that represent fundamental principles are these:

- *Access.* This is, it seems to me, about as fundamental as a library principle can get. If the library isn't giving anyone access to information, then it's hard to see why it exists, or even how it can meaningfully be considered a library. Indeed, I would say that access is more fundamental than collections—because collections exist for the purpose of supporting access, not the other way around.
- *Intellectual freedom.* This value contemplates how and why we impose structure on access. We can impose structure for the purpose of enhancing access (by, for example, putting time limits on circulation so as to help ensure that everyone will get a chance to use the library's resources), but we could also impose structure for the purpose of restricting access (by, for example, limiting access to materials that we or some group of patrons consider offensive). Libraries invariably impose structure on their collections and on their service models, but it is a core value and a fundamental principle of libraries that we try always to impose structure in ways that enhance, rather than restrict, our patrons' ability to read what they wish.
- *Service.* Everything we do is (or should be) built on a foundation of service. A library without service is nothing but a collection of documents sitting in a building.

Subordinate Principles

Values that represent subordinate principles are not necessarily less important than those representing fundamental principles, but they are subordinate in that their importance lies in their service to fundamental principles, with which they should not be confused.

Looking at the ALA's list of core values, it seems to me that the following represent subordinate principles:

- *Confidentiality/privacy* (which protects intellectual freedom)
- *Diversity* (which improves service quality, helps ensure equitable access, and enhances intellectual freedom)

- *Professionalism* (which should characterize our services)
- *Preservation* (the purpose of which is to ensure continued access)

There is real danger in confusing fundamental principles with subordinate ones. I once had a very interesting discussion with a colleague who believed that it would be wrong for the library to offer access to any resource that required end users to provide basic personal information, such as an e-mail address, even if the resource was in very high demand. My colleague believed that for the library to offer such a resource would constitute a breach of our patrons' privacy. But one could equally argue that failing to offer it undermines access, service quality, and perhaps even (more alarmingly) our patrons' intellectual freedom.[2] By restricting access to the resource in question, the library is effectively saying to the patron, "We know better than you do how much you should value your privacy, and we're going to protect you from yourself by not giving you the option of making what we think would be a bad privacy decision." This is not to downplay the importance of privacy, of course. But *when two core values come into conflict, you need a way of deciding which one will win.* Knowing which one you consider a fundamental principle and which you consider subordinate can help with that decision.

Questionable "Core Values"

Now comes the harder part. Here are the items from the ALA's "core values" list that strike me as problematic—certainly not bad or wrong in and of themselves, but troublesome in that their real-world application as core values seems unclear or because they may conflict with other values that we also consider "core":

- *Education and lifelong learning.* These are clearly good and important things. But can they reasonably be characterized as core values of librarianship? If so, why would any library spend scarce resources on recreational books or films that provide little, if any, educational value?
- *Democracy.* Most of us in libraries will agree, I'm sure, that democracy is a good thing. But how do we square the institutional endorsement of one particular political and social philosophy with core values of intellectual freedom and diversity? There are some in the communities we serve (at both the liberal and the conservative ends of the political/philosophical spectrum) who question whether democratic political systems are best for society. If we consider democracy a core value of librarianship,

then how should the library serve a patron who is doing research in support of explicitly anti-democratic political goals? In other words, how can we say that democracy, diversity, and intellectual freedom are all simultaneously core values of librarianship?

- *Social responsibility.* In the abstract, this is certainly an important principle. However, unless everyone in our profession thinks and believes the same things (which will not be the case if we truly value diversity), "social responsibility" will be understood so differently by so many different librarians that it's hard to see what it can actually mean in professional practice. Pick virtually any social issue—gun control; educational reform; the proper definition of marriage; tax policy—and a meaningfully diverse profession (not to mention its constituency of patrons) will harbor a wide variety of views on what constitutes socially responsible action. If we truly consider diversity and intellectual freedom to be core values of librarianship, then our profession is in a bad position to push any specific social agenda—and "social responsibility" without a specific social agenda is meaningless.
- *The public good.* The problem with this value is not that it is in any way controversial in and of itself, but rather that it is so vague and so purely subjective. As a core value, it poses the same problem that "social responsibility" does: How can "the public good" represent a professional core value if a meaningfully diverse profession will inevitably disagree on what best serves the public good?

In closing, let me reiterate: my purpose here is not to suggest that any of the items in the ALA's "core values" list is in any way unworthy or objectionable. But taken as a whole, the list has a problem: one of the hard things about life in the real world is that two things can be simultaneously good and mutually incompatible. If our profession's formally declared values statement is going to be defensible, it must be coherent. And for it to be coherent, its internal contradictions will need, in some way, to be addressed and dealt with.

NOTES

1.   American Library Association, "Core Values of Librarianship" (adopted June 29, 2004), www.ala.org/advocacy/intfreedom/statementspols/corevalues.

2.   For further discussion of this argument, see essay 7 in this volume.

12

Asserting Rights We Don't Have

Libraries and "Permission to Publish"

IN JUNE 2014, a minor brouhaha erupted when the library at the University of Arkansas suspended reporters from the *Washington Free Beacon*, an online newspaper, from using its special collections. The reason given by library administrators was that on multiple occasions the newspaper's reporters had published content from those collections without asking permission, as library policy requires. Much has been made in the right-wing press about the politics supposedly surrounding this conflict: in the incident that resulted in the *Free Beacon*'s ban, it had published interview transcripts that put Hillary Clinton in a bad light; the *Free Beacon* is a conservative publication, and the library dean is reportedly a donor to the Clinton Foundation. But while the political issues in this particular case are interesting and may be worthy of discussion, I want to focus on a different issue: the practice of making patrons request library permission before republishing (in whole or in part) content drawn from documents in our special collections.

It's in the nature of special collections that their holdings are, well, special. They generally include not only formally and commercially published documents that are rare or highly valuable, or that have a particular relevance to the host institution, but also rare and unique unpublished documents in a variety of formats. Some of these will be under copyright (as is the case with the tape recordings from the University of Arkansas's library); others will be in the public domain. In the case of documents that are under copyright, it's relatively rare—

This essay was originally published in *Library Journal*'s *Academic Newswire*, August 21, 2014. Reprinted by permission.

though not unheard of—for the holding library to be the copyright holder.

Where the library is the copyright holder, the library is completely within its rights to require patrons to ask permission before making use of the documents in question that goes beyond fair use. And where the document is under a copyright held by someone other than the library, it makes sense for the library to let patrons know that the law puts certain limits on their use of the document. If the materials have been donated or lent to the library under restrictive terms, the library is of course obliged to abide by those restrictions as well.

What is much less clear to me is how a library can justify (in the absence of a donor restriction) requiring patrons to ask permission to make lawful use of intellectual content that is in the public domain. Such requirements appear to be quite standard in academic libraries; you'll find "permission to publish" requirements at Willamette University, at Stanford, at Arizona State University, and at the University of Utah (my own institution), among many others. Some libraries (for example, Princeton's) require patrons to ask permission before even quoting from documents housed in their special collections, even if those documents are in the public domain.

Such requirements are not universal, however. At the University of Virginia, the library's special collections department explicitly disavows such restrictions, saying that "it is not necessary to seek the Library's permission as the owner of the physical work to publish or otherwise use public domain materials that the Library has made available online from its collections," adding that it is the "sole responsibility of the user . . . to investigate the copyright status of any given work and to seek and obtain permission where needed prior to any distribution or publication."[1] The Harvard Law Library does so as well (though only for documents dating before 1850), and so does the University of Wisconsin (though its policy document is a bit confusing).

Does a library have the legal right to impose such restrictions on reuse of public-domain content? Strictly speaking, no: physical ownership of a public-domain document does not give the owner the right to say how the document's content may be used. However, what the owner of the physical document certainly may do is control access to it. Even a public university has the right to control access to its collections, especially collections that are fragile, unique, or otherwise in need of special care. There's nothing illegal about saying, "You may not have physical access to our rare and unique materials unless you are willing to agree to use them under terms that we set." There is also nothing illegal about saying (as the University of Arkansas did to the *Free Beacon* reporters), "If you don't abide by our terms of access and reuse, we will stop letting you have access to our collections."

But my question isn't really about the library's legal rights. It's about whether we're abiding by the principles we claim as being core to our profession—in particular, those principles related to intellectual freedom, the public good, and service. It's one thing to require that rare or fragile documents be handled carefully and under supervision, and it's one thing to educate patrons about copyright law; it's quite another thing to require that patrons ask our permission before reusing the intellectual content of documents in the public domain, and even (as many libraries do) to inform us ahead of time how they plan to use it. When we require them to ask our permission before republishing, quoting, or otherwise reusing public-domain content, we are asserting a right we don't have—the right to control our patrons' use of public intellectual property. We would never consider trying to impose that kind of control over our patrons' use of public-domain content from our general collections, so what is it about rare and unique materials that makes us think it's okay to do so in that context?

I posed that question to several special collections librarians whose programs require patrons to ask permission to publish or quote from public-domain documents. Some of the answers I got had to do with the difficulty of managing materials that have been given to the library under restrictive terms. In such cases, the issue isn't copyright but, rather, one of abiding by the agreements made when the gift or loan was accepted. Someone might donate an ancestor's diary to the library with the understanding that it will only be made available to researchers in certain very specific ways. Donors are, again, completely within their rights to impose such conditions, and libraries that accept the donations are obliged to abide by them. As one librarian pointed out to me, the permission-to-publish form provides a practical mechanism for prompting library staff to check and make sure such restrictions aren't in place before allowing the republication of this kind of material. However, this seems to me like something of a cart-before-the-horse arrangement. Instead of a system that requires patrons to fill out forms and then requires staff to consult deeds of gift every time someone wants to make lawful use of public-domain content, shouldn't such restrictions be recorded in registers and finding aids as part of the processing of every gift? Patrons can't usually locate special collections materials unless finding aids for those materials have been created—shouldn't the creation of those finding aids include annotations about donor restrictions?

Other responses I got were far less satisfactory. One librarian seemed not to understand some basic points of copyright law—for example, the fact that a library can't claim copyright in the unaltered digital image of a public-domain document. Some sought to justify their "permission to publish" requirements on the basis of the library's need to track usage of content from its collections, in order to provide justification for the special collections program; others did so on the basis of being able to charge usage fees for commercial reuse or said that mediating access to the content puts the librarian in a position to educate the user on copyright issues.

For the most part, these strike me as remarkably weak justifications for imposing an entirely artificial restriction on our patrons' legal reuse of public-domain content—for acting, in short, as if our ownership of physical copies of these documents entitles us to limit and control the use of those documents' intellectual content. Again: This isn't an issue of legal rights, strictly speaking; if we own a copy of a document, there's nothing technically illegal about denying someone physical access to that copy for any reason we care to come up with, even if the document's intellectual content is in the public domain. This is an issue of professional standards and ethics. As a profession that proclaims loudly and often its support for the free and open sharing of information—one that, in fact, regularly calls for the free distribution and unrestricted reuse of documents arising from publicly funded research—how can we, with a straight face, make people ask our permission to exercise the rights of redistribution and reuse that the law provides them, whether for private, public, commercial, or noncommercial purposes? And as a profession that proclaims its support for principles of intellectual freedom, how can we justify asking patrons to tell us, ahead of time, in what kind of publications and for what purposes they intend to republish public-domain content?

Based on the conversations I've had with my colleagues in preparing this column, these seem to be questions that make us uncomfortable. So be it. Let's have the conversation anyway.

NOTE

1.   Albert and Shirley Small Special Collections Library, "Publishing Materials from the Library's Collections" (Charlottesville, VA: The University of Virginia), https://small.library.virginia.edu/services/reproduction/publishing.

13

Frenemies

The Perfect and the Good,
the Noisy and the Important

The Perfect and the Good

WE'VE ALL HEARD—and many of us have probably invoked ourselves—the admonition "Don't let the perfect be the enemy of the good." It's a concept that has a kind of fraught history in library discourse because it embodies a tension that exists between two conflicting aspects of library culture: on the one hand, we place a lot of value on accuracy, completeness, and quality in the work that we do; on the other hand, we are painfully aware of the limited resources with which we have to work.

The tension between these two realities is sometimes expressed in the form of conflict between those who invoke the phrase "Don't let the perfect be the enemy of the good" and those who hear it. Those who use it may be urging the hearers to get a particular task to the point of "good enough" and then move on to other tasks that also need to be addressed. They also may invoke this concept in order to send the message that we shouldn't let our inability to do something perfectly stop us from doing it at all.

In both of the above contexts, I would suggest that this slogan makes good sense and that it stands in explicit opposition to another

---

This essay was originally published as two columns in *Library Journal*'s *Academic Newswire*, September 18 and December 4, 2014. Reprinted by permission.

familiar saying: "If a thing is worth doing, it's worth doing well." Not all necessary tasks are equally important. This means that, in fact, all things that have to be done are not worth doing equally well; some things are worth doing just well enough to get them off your desk or your to-do list, so that you can turn your attention to more important work. In this sense, "not letting the perfect be the enemy of the good" means recognizing the important principle of opportunity cost: since our time and energy are limited, any task we undertake comes at the cost of other tasks that thereby fall by the wayside. If our time and energy were unlimited, it would be appropriate to aspire to do everything and to do it all perfectly, but since both are strictly limited, we have to make decisions—sometimes wrenching ones—not only about what we will and won't do but also about what we'll take the time to do really well and what we'll do less well so that we can move on to projects of greater value and importance.

On the other hand, "not letting the perfect be the enemy of the good" can also be a cop-out, an excuse used by people who can't be bothered to improve their performance or to deliver really good service. If we invoke the slogan in defense of laziness ("Don't push me to improve my skills") or organizational inertia ("We're already doing enough to help our patrons and our institution"), then I would suggest that we're misusing it.

So the principle of "not letting the perfect be the enemy of the good" has much to recommend it, but like virtually every principle, it can be applied both appropriately and inappropriately. I'd like to suggest two rules of thumb for applying it well:

First, apply it where the question is, "Does Proposition X result in a net gain in efficiency or effectiveness?" In other words, we shouldn't forego a program that would make things better just because it won't make things perfect. Sometimes we experience opposition to new ideas on just this basis. Someone suggests that we create an institutional repository (IR) that will make the scholarship produced on campus more fully available to the general public, and someone else— someone who, perhaps, might not want to undertake the significant work it would require—says, "Look, our establishment of an IR isn't going to solve the problem of access to scholarship." (Of course it won't, and no one is arguing that it would. The argument is that establishing and maintaining an IR would generate benefits equal to or greater than the cost of doing so.) In other words, the fact that a proposed program doesn't create perfection does not mean that it doesn't achieve enough good to be worth doing.

The principle should also be applied where tasks or practices need to be done to a functional level of quality or completeness in order to achieve an important goal but where levels of quality above the functional return little or no marginal benefit. This is the sense in which the principle is often applied in the context of cataloging: How many subject headings does a record really need to have in order for the item to be findable in the catalog? Catalog records need to be as complete and accurate as necessary, not as complete and accurate as possible.

Second rule of thumb: ignore this principle where the question is, "Does Proposition X get us as close to our goals of efficiency or effectiveness as we need to be?" If the proposition in question is designed to get us closer to perfection in an area where something close to perfection is truly needed, then the principle of "not letting the perfect be the enemy of the good" should go out the window. This begs an important question: Are there areas of library work in which we really should be striving for perfection, or for something as close to it as we can get? Yes, I believe so. The personal service that we provide on reference desks; the salience and clarity of library signage; the accuracy and completeness of our financial accounting; our integrity as employees and leaders—all of these, it seems to me, deserve constant attention, may need constant improvement, and allow for little, if any, compromise.

The Noisy and the Important

Of course, no matter what our approach to decision-making and prioritization, the constant danger is that we won't make such decisions carefully and mindfully but will instead fall prey to the temptation to give full attention to the issues and problems that are noisiest, that are brought to us by the people with the strongest personalities, that appeal to our personal biases and preferences, or that otherwise present themselves to us in ways that make giving our time and attention to them the course of least resistance.

In such cases, the temptation is to let the noisy be the enemy of the important. The problem we face is that not all needs and problems are equally "noisy," and it can be easy to mistake noisiness for importance. In order to explain what I mean by that, let me start by going off on a tangent.

As a manager or administrator, you have to have (among others) two particular kinds of character strength. The first is *the strength to hear good ideas and arguments when they're presented by obnoxious people.* When you're trying to solve problems or improve services or create and maintain effective programs, you need to be able to hear and recognize good ideas and arguments regardless of whether they come from people who make themselves pleasant to deal with. This is not easy; when someone is a jerk, one of the easiest ways to deal with him is simply to push him to the margins and tune him out. That's often a mistake, for several reasons. One is that good ideas are no less likely to come from difficult people than from pleasant ones; another is that sometimes what makes a person difficult to deal with is that person's ability and willingness to question comfortable assumptions and well-established processes—which is an important and objectively valuable ability in any organization.

Some leaders seem to understand this intuitively and do a good job of making sure that people with difficult personalities are given a chance to have their voices heard and their ideas evaluated fairly. When doing so, however, it's important to bring into play the second kind of character strength I want to examine. This one is almost the mirror image of the first: it's *the ability to resist being swayed by ideas and arguments just because they're being presented by strong personalities.* When an argument or idea is being pushed at you hard by someone who believes in it passionately and is clearly willing to make your life difficult if you reject it, one easy response is to push that person away, but another easy response is simply to let that person have his way. That, too, is often a mistake—not because his idea is necessarily bad (see above), but because when leaders make organizational decisions based on the desire to ease their own discomfort, they usually end up getting short-term relief at the cost of long-term dysfunction.

And this brings us back to the very significant distinction between "noisy" problems and important ones.

Obnoxious interpersonal behavior is a form of noise: the abrasiveness of the delivery tends to distract our attention from the relevant content of what is being delivered.

Aggressive advocacy is also a form of noise: the urgency and passion of the person doing the advocating may tell us quite a bit about that person's enthusiasm and commitment, but they don't necessarily say anything at all (one way or the other) about whether the idea is worth pursuing and implementing.

One of the constant challenges facing leaders and managers in libraries is separating the "noisiness" of a problem from its importance. This difficulty is compounded because some very serious problems may not be noisy at all; they may be causing serious trouble without anyone noticing (at first) or drawing attention to them. A small and unnoticed water leak inside your wall can, over time, cause tens of thousands of dollars in damage, whereas a sudden power outage may distract all of your attention in the moment without causing any long-term problem. We see a similar dynamic in our libraries: "quiet" problems can percolate along for years, causing serious harm to the library's effectiveness and reputation, while "noisy" ones can cause distraction far out of proportion to their real importance.

Consider these two scenarios:

More noisy but less important: A patron sends multiple e-mail messages to the head of collection development, insisting that the library purchase his self-published book on the government's conspiracy to suppress evidence of UFOs. When the collection development librarian declines to do so, the author demands to meet with the library director, then with the provost. This situation may generate a fair amount of noise but probably doesn't represent a serious problem for the library or its patrons.

More important but less noisy: Patrons can't find known items in the catalog because a setting in the discovery layer is putting the wrong items at the top of the search results. If patrons assume that the library simply doesn't have what they're looking for (and therefore don't follow up with requests for help), this problem may generate little, if any, noise. But over time, if unaddressed, it will significantly degrade both the library's effectiveness and its reputation.

These scenarios suggest that just because a problem is noisy doesn't mean it's important and vice versa. But none of this is to say that noisiness is a completely irrelevant consideration; it may be very important, depending on the nature of the noise and the politics surrounding the issue. But while noise may have serious political implications, it is almost always a poor indicator of mission implications. In other words, a noisy problem may need to be addressed quickly because it threatens to cause serious public relations concerns—you don't want people going to the provost to complain about the library, regardless of how silly their complaints may be—but those considerations have little to do with whether the issue at hand has anything intrinsically to do with the library's effectiveness at fulfilling its mission and goals. So rather than saying some problems are noisy but unimportant, it might be better to say that noisiness is not always a good indicator of importance—and that we can never assume that the amount of noise (whether great or small) generated by a problem is directly proportional to its significance.

14

What Patron-Driven Acquisition Does and Doesn't Mean

An FAQ

OVER THE PAST couple of years I've been writing and presenting pretty relentlessly on the topic of patron-driven acquisition (PDA) in research libraries, arguing that in a predominantly online information environment, it no longer fundamentally makes sense for most academic libraries to build large permanent collections based on librarians' speculations about patrons' future needs. For one thing, our speculations are very often wrong; for another, the combination of shrinking budgets and relentlessly increasing prices (especially for scholarly journals) makes traditional collection practices decreasingly feasible from a purely economic standpoint—we just can't afford to keep building collections the way we have in the past.

PDA is built on a deceptively simple premise: in a largely digital information environment, it's increasingly possible to let library users find and identify desired documents prior to the library's purchase of them, and for the library to pay only for what its patrons find and actually use. When a patron's use of an e-book or a journal article passes a certain agreed-upon threshold (a certain number of e-book pages read, for example, or the download of a complete article), the library is charged, the document acquired, and the patron never knows that the document was not part of the "collection" to begin with. Such an arrangement has the potential to be enormously liberating for library

This essay was originally published in *The Scholarly Kitchen* (blog), May 31, 2011.

users, and to solve one of the library's long-standing and fundamental problems: the fact that traditional "just-in-case" collections give patrons access to only a tiny (and inconsistently relevant) sliver of the population of documents that are actually available for use.

But like all acquisition and access models, PDA is imperfect, its manifestations are numerous and to some degree chaotic, and its availability raises lots and lots of questions, many of which I find myself trying to answer during the Q&A segments at the ends of my presentations. Several questions arise repeatedly, which suggests to me that there's broad interest in answers to them. Here are some of those questions, with my attempts at responses.

Q: Isn't *all* collection development patron-driven? After all, librarians have always striven to understand patrons' needs and take them into account when selecting materials for the collection.

A: In academic libraries, we've gotten very good at understanding our patrons' needs in the aggregate: we know the curriculum and we know our faculties and their areas of research interest, and that knowledge has always guided our collecting strategies. This means, for example, that it's possible for me to know that my faculty needs good books on high-energy physics. The problem is that it's not possible to buy "books on high-energy physics." It's only possible to buy *specific* books on high-energy physics, which necessarily entails *not* buying other books on high-energy physics, and my ability to predict *which exact books on high-energy physics* my patrons will need and use is very limited. Remember that the purpose of the collection isn't to be a great collection; it's to connect patrons with exactly what they need (see further discussion of the collection's purpose below).

Q: Is it really our job to just "give the people what they want"?

A: Where "the people" are the students and faculty members we're being paid to serve, and where "what they want" are resources that support their scholarly work, then I think the short answer to this question is, "Yes, that's exactly our job." The obvious corollary to this question is, "But what if all they want is comic books and genre fiction?" The answer to that is while PDA can offer a technically unlimited array of options to our patrons, fiscal reality makes some limitations inevitable. We may have to filter the options we show them. Depending on our institutional mission, we might exclude romance fiction or travel guides from the range of options, for example (while leaving the door open to special requests from researchers working in popular culture or related fields). As long as resources are limited, no access model will be perfect.

Q: How will PDA help me save money?

A: It probably won't. And to my mind, that's fine. I have no expectation that PDA will allow me to spend less money on books and articles; I expect it only to help ensure that all the money I do spend will go to materials that my patrons actually need. Don't get me wrong; I love to save money. But that's not why I do PDA.

Q: How can you say that *any* purchase is a "waste of money"? You yourself said that we never know perfectly what our patrons are going to need in the future.

A: That's true, but since it's true of absolutely any document—there is no document about which you can't say "someday someone might need access to this"—it doesn't help me make good decisions about my use of limited resources. Unless I have an unlimited budget, I have to choose between multiple potentially useful documents, and that means I have to try to pick the ones that are most likely to be used. And my patrons can do that much more effectively than I can.

Q: Won't PDA hurt publishers?

A: Yes, and that's unfortunate. I mean that sincerely. But we have a problem, and the problem is that the current publishing marketplace evolved in an environment in which library customers had no choice but to buy lots of books and articles that they didn't need because that was the only way to guarantee access to books and articles that they did need. That's not a criticism of publishers; it's a criticism of the print-based information environment. PDA has the potential to make the information marketplace much more efficient and rational, which means that publishers will go out of business to the degree that they relied (however unintentionally) on marketplace inefficiencies to keep them in business. I wish that weren't the case, but it is.

Q: PDA always seems to be about books. Doesn't the same principle apply to journals?

A: Absolutely. The journal subscription is a fundamentally irrational way to buy access to articles; it involves buying lots of content you don't need in order to ensure access to some content that you do need (while excluding other big batches of content, which may also contain articles you need). PDA principles apply to journal content at the article level:

ideally, libraries should expose huge and comprehensive "collections" of unacquired journal articles to their patrons and buy only those that their patrons actually download. A certain number of paid downloads should result in permanent site-wide access (on the assumption that multiple uses of a single article demonstrates broad need on that campus). The details of such an arrangement would have to be a matter of negotiation with the publisher; the most important detail, obviously, will be price per article.

Q: How do you control your spending in a PDA environment?

A: This is a huge issue, and it's one that is being handled in a variety of ways from both sides of the supply-demand divide. One possibility is to use a "risk pool" approach as a throttle mechanism: if the rate of purchase is outstripping the budget, then the number of books offered for PDA is reduced until demand slows. On the supply side, publishers and aggregators generally offer management tools that make it relatively easy to track usage activity in real time, and to tighten or relax access as needed. In the article environment, it might make sense simply to ration the number of permitted downloads. We should expect that publishers and aggregators will compete with each other, in part, on the basis of their ability to help us manage spending, so we should probably not expect a one-size-fits-all solution to emerge.

Q: My library subscribes to several comprehensive journal packages from major science publishers. The pricing for these packages is advantageous enough that buying the articles one by one would result in a much higher expenditure than simply sticking with the Big Deal does. Surely a PDA approach doesn't make sense in my case.

A: It's true that a Big Deal will often result in very low per-download costs. But that doesn't mean that it makes sense to buy a huge batch of articles, only some of which will get used; it means only that the publisher has set pricing in such a way as to discourage per-article purchasing and encourage bulk purchasing. Such arrangements may be attractive in the short run, but they are objectively unsustainable in the long run. The Big Deal was not (*pace* Derk Haank) a solution to the serials pricing crisis—it was only a way of kicking the can of unsustainable pricing down the road for a few years.[1]

Q: How can you build a great collection if you buy only what today's patrons want? Won't the result be a rather haphazard, possibly even incoherent pile of content rather than a well-rounded, intelligently shaped research collection?

A: This goes to a fundamental philosophical issue on which I and many of my colleagues disagree. I believe it's essential to the survival of academic libraries that we learn to see the collection as a means, not an end. By this reasoning, an arguably fine (i.e., high-quality, well-organized, and reasonably comprehensive) collection that fails to meet the actual real-life needs of the scholarly population it is supposed to serve is not a "good" collection in any meaningful sense. In fact, I'm not sure we can safely assume that building collections is still the right way to go about meeting patrons' information needs at all. While it probably makes sense for a few richly funded research libraries to build and maintain huge and comprehensive collections (I call these the Monument to Western Civilization collections), for the vast majority of academic libraries that kind of collecting has always been impossible and is now increasingly irrational.

NOTE

1, Richard Poynder, "Interview with Springer's Derk Haank," *Open and Shut?* (blog), January 14, 2011, http://poynder.blogspot.com/2011/01/interview-with-springers-derk-haank.html.

15

Reference Services, Scalability, and the Starfish Problem

HERE'S A FAMILIAR inspirational story: A man is walking on the beach and discovers thousands of starfish, stranded and dying above the waterline. There are far more than he can possibly hope to rescue on his own, but he begins, implacably, to pick them up one at a time and throw them as far as he can back into the water. Soon another man comes along and sees what he's doing. He watches for a while and then says, "You know, there are too many of them. It's not going to make any difference." The first man looks down at the starfish in his hand and responds, "It makes a difference to this one."

The moral of the story is that even if our individual efforts can't change everything, they can change something, and each of us can make a great difference to other individuals who need our help. It's a wonderful analogy, but it depends for its power on one important but unspoken assumption: the man in the story is a volunteer, helping starfish on his own time. If he were employed by the state to solve the problem of starfish getting stranded on the beach, and if he were going about his assignment by throwing them back one by one, then the story wouldn't be an illustration of praiseworthy altruism. It would be an illustration of incompetence, featuring a man who should be fired.

One of the dangerous things about being a librarian is the opportunity it gives us to help people. I realize that sounds crazy, so let me explain: This morning I was on my way to a meeting. As I hurried down the hall, I noticed a student looking confused and sort of wandering in a circle near the book stacks. Although I was running a little bit late, I

This essay was originally published in *Against the Grain* 19, no. 5 (November 2007): 16.

couldn't stand to pass her by without offering some help, so I asked if she needed a hand. It turned out that she was having a hard time figuring out the call number she had written down—she was confused by the decimal places and had ended up in the wrong section of shelving. ("These numbers are so confusing," she muttered at one point.) It took us a few minutes to get everything straightened out, but I finally got her to the right place and she found her book and thanked me profusely. I continued on to my meeting with a spring in my step. I had really helped someone, and she had really appreciated it, and life was good. But the man with the starfish kept coming into my mind and making me feel uneasy.

Why? Because one major area of traditional librarianship—reference service—is built on a fundamentally flawed model, and it's a model that reinforces itself by making us feel good when we implement it. We sit at desks or encounter patrons in the stacks, and we interact with our users one-on-one. Most of those interactions are quick and shallow and amount to directional help, and the more such interactions we have with patrons, the more uneasy we get. If you spend an hour telling people where the bathrooms are, you're inevitably going to start asking yourself uncomfortable questions about whether your time is being well spent. But then a patron approaches with a deep and involved research problem, and he draws on your expertise in gratifying ways, and sometimes the help you give makes a very large (maybe even a life-changing) impact. You feel wonderful after these experiences. "This is what librarianship is all about!," you say to yourself. And so you continue doing it, and you get better and better at it, and you train others to do it well also.

And the more we do it, the better we feel, and the less inclined we are to address the bigger, more intractable problem: the fact that this model of patron service will inevitably leave the vast majority of our patrons unserved. The calculus is cruel but undeniable: fifteen minutes spent by one librarian helping one patron gives a miserable return on the money spent by the librarian's employer—an investment that is, in most cases, intended to help thousands and thousands of patrons. For every library user who comes to our reference desks or tugs on our sleeves in the stacks, there are hundreds or even thousands who have similar needs and never get any help at all. I know for a fact that this bothers many of us, but I don't think it bothers most of us nearly as much as it should.

To me, what felt like the key moment in my interaction with a library patron this morning was the moment that she found the book and thanked me effusively. I had helped her find her book! She was thrilled! So was I! And if I had been a volunteer looking for a way to be of help to someone, I'd be absolutely right to feel wonderful about what I'd done. But I'm not a volunteer, and I wasn't investing my own time. I'm being paid to help 29,000 students, and I was investing my employer's time.

Should I have declined to help her? Of course not. But it's important to think clearly about the significance of our interaction. The key moment did not come when we found the book and she thanked me for all my fine help. Rather, *it came when she muttered, "These numbers are so confusing."* The crux of her problem lay in the fact that LC call numbers look like gibberish to most normal people, and that libraries themselves are still, despite our ongoing efforts, very difficult to use. I'd be willing to bet money that a very large proportion of the 29,000 students served by my library find LC call numbers just as confusing as she did, and I can promise you that most of them will never have the kind of interaction with a librarian that she had with me. This isn't because we librarians aren't willing to have those conversations or aren't good at having those conversations, but simply because there are too many of them and too few of us. In an academic or large public library, traditional reference service is simply not scalable to the size of the patron population that needs our help.

Again: Am I suggesting that we stop offering one-on-one service to our patrons? Absolutely not. As long as patrons keep coming to our reference desks, there need to be people there waiting to help them. But in the short run, I believe we need to think long and hard about how that kind of service should fit into our libraries' structures and what we're going to do about the fact that it's available to so few of the people we serve. In the long run, we should be trying to put our reference desks out of business. We need to design our services so that they serve *all* of our patrons well—not just the small minority of patrons who approach our service desks looking for help. To some degree, we do this already when we shift print resources to online, and when we provide online help, and when we figure out ways to make access more intuitive so that patrons can get what they need without having to find someone to help them.

But I think we can (and must) do more. We need to radically rethink the catalog and make it simpler—less exhaustively complete, less painstakingly accurate, more timely and more user-friendly—so that patrons actually need less help in using it. We should take a very hardheaded look at how time is spent on reference desks, especially by highly paid, expensively trained librarians. How many patrons does a librarian actually get to help in a typical hour of desk time? Could that hour be more fruitfully spent in front of a class somewhere else on campus or consulting with a professor or a department head on ways to better integrate library services with the curriculum? If the vast majority of questions fielded at a reference desk are directional or otherwise routine, doesn't it make sense to staff the desk with less expensive and less specifically expert personnel, who can refer patrons to librarians as needed? Please note that none of this is to question the value of reference librarians; on the contrary, it's the very high value of reference librarians that makes me question traditional reference service. In other words, what I'm questioning is whether we're using reference librarians the right way and whether our patrons are getting the tremendous benefits that reference librarians can offer.

The root of my patron's problem lay in the fact that the library is hard to use. I helped her find a book, but I didn't solve her problem—even if it seemed to both of us like I did. The problem with traditional reference service is that it isn't scalable, and the solution to that problem does not lie in improving or expanding reference service but, rather, in making traditional reference service less necessary. If only it didn't feel so good to provide traditional reference services, we might be more motivated to try harder to put our desks out of business.

16

Kitten in a Beer Mug

The Myth of the Free Gift

MOST OF US WHO work in libraries are familiar with the Myth of the Free Gift—otherwise known as the Kittens-or-Beer Conundrum.

If you work in acquisitions or collection development, you've almost certainly been approached by someone whose parent recently died and left behind a collection of several hundred chemistry texts or political science monographs from the 1950s—these will be described to you as a "priceless collection of scholarly books"—which the donor can't bring himself to throw away and which he believes should therefore be given a home in your library. If you hesitate, the donor will be shocked and maybe even offended. You're a library, after all, and these priceless books are being offered to you for free. Why wouldn't you want them?

If you work in public services, you've probably experienced a variation on this scenario in the form of volunteers: people who show up at the library and offer their services at no charge and can't understand why you might hesitate to take them up on the offer.

Now, I want to be very clear: gift books can be wonderful, and volunteers often perform incredibly valuable service in our libraries. We love and appreciate both of them. But they illustrate the absolutely vital difference between Free Beer and Free Kittens.

Free beer is a gift that requires nothing of us but to consume it. Unrestricted cash donations are free beer. Even restricted money— money that can be used only for purposes specified by the donor—is free beer, as long as the strings attached to it don't create added work or aggravation for the library.

This essay was originally published in *Library Journal's Academic Newswire*, September 19, 2013. Reprinted by permission.

Just about every other kind of donation, whether it be a donation of goods or a donation of labor, is free kittens. Free kittens don't cost anything to acquire, but they entail ongoing costs as you keep and care for them. Donated books have to be searched, deduped, reviewed, cataloged, and physically processed before they can be added to the collection—where they will take up shelf space and require some degree of ongoing care. Volunteers, obviously, require both training and supervision—and since they're volunteers, they're liable to turn over more frequently than regular employees, thus requiring more investment in training. The costs involved with accepting gifts and hosting volunteers may be well worth it, just as the cost of feeding and caring for a kitten may be worth it. But the fact that the costs are worth it doesn't make the costs less real or make it less necessary to give them careful consideration.

Furthermore, the downstream costs of accepting gifts of goods or labor are not always obvious up front—especially not to the people offering them, who often believe they're giving you free beer. Look in the mug, though, and what you'll almost always find is a kitten.

Even healthy kittens are expensive to care for, and not all healthy-looking kittens are actually healthy. Some kittens look cute and cuddly when they arrive in your home but then turn out to be not only unhealthy but also dangerous. Look carefully at the splotches on the pages of that eighteenth-century book that was just donated to your library: Do they represent harmless foxing, or are they a colony of toxic mold that will make your staff ill when they try to process the book? (Hard experience has taught me the importance of asking this question.)

Some kittens are criminals: Are you positive that the donor who is offering you a collection of books actually has the right to give it to you? Those who work in special collections departments are used to asking provenance questions because they are often dealing with rare and unique documents, but this can be an important and fraught issue with general collection materials as well (as I have also learned by painful experience).

Some kittens are being offered for foster care, not adoption: Does your library use a carefully worded Deed of Gift document that makes clear the nature of each gift and that (once signed by the donor) leaves the library with clear ownership of the material and the right to dispose of it as the library sees fit? If not, then you run the risk of having the donor change his or her mind about the terms of transfer later on or object to the way in which you're managing the gift and push you to do it in some other way.

Some kittens are zombies: accepting a donation of microfiche, eight-track tapes, cassettes, or documents in other outdated or moribund formats will often amount to inviting a cadre of the undead into your library, where they will lurk awkwardly about the edges of your collection, silently pleading for inclusion in a working, living collection that has no practical way of integrating them.

Kittens always need special attention: unlike the ones that we buy from vendors, donated books can't be made to come to us "shelf-ready." This means that in some cases, it may be more expensive to accept a book as a gift than it would be to buy a copy commercially.

The key to dealing with these kinds of challenges is to decide well ahead of time how and under what circumstances you're willing to adopt kittens. If your library doesn't already have formal policies that govern the acceptance of gift materials and the management of volunteers, establish them. Your policies should provide answers to questions such as these:

- What formats will we accept, and why do we have restrictions?
- What subject areas are in and out of scope for us?
- What areas of the library are open to volunteer service, and which ones are not?
- What rights do volunteers have, and what obligations does the library have to them?
- What rights do we require donors to give the library along with the materials themselves?
- What will we do with donated books that don't end up being added to the collection?
- Under what circumstances (if at all) will we send library staff to pick up donations?
- How many hours of volunteer labor can the library absorb?
- Do we assess the value of gifts for tax purposes? (Hint: the answer to this question is, "No.")
- Who may supervise volunteers, and how will volunteer labor be tracked and accounted for?

One particularly nice thing about having a policy in place is that it gives your frontline staff a backstop when they are dealing with a difficult would-be donor. For staff, it's much easier to say to a donor, "I'm so sorry, but these materials fall outside the parameters of our gift policy" than to say, "Hmmm, I don't think these look like a good fit for our collection." For the public, it's much harder to argue with an established, documented, well-defined policy than with a staff member expressing an opinion.

One important caveat: sometimes gifts will be offered by people whom you wish to make happy for reasons that have nothing to do with the gift itself. If a major donor to the library's (or the university's) general fund offers you a gift of 200 eight-track tapes from 1973, it may be wise to accept that gift with a big and sincere smile. In a case like this, the cost of accepting the gift may be outweighed by the value of maintaining and deepening the library's relationship with that donor. In other words, sometimes you do have to make room in your home for a zombie kitten. Just don't expect it to act like beer.

17

You Might Be a Zealot If . . .

LIKE MANY OF US who work in acquisitions, collection development, serials, and publishing, I interact with lots of people from all over the scholarly information world: librarians, library staff, students, publishers, editors, authors, sales reps, consortium officers, etc. As a group, we have a wide variety of views on issues like publishing and pricing models, cataloging, open access, peer review, collection development, customer service, etc. And almost all of us are reasonable, intelligent people of good faith who want to find workable solutions to real-world problems and are willing to work cooperatively with one another to get to those solutions.

But occasionally we run into a zealot. You know what I mean: a person who is not so much dedicated to finding solutions to problems as to convincing everyone of the One True Solution to every problem—or, conversely, to warning everyone about an Impending and Apocalyptic Danger.

The chief characteristics of zealotry, it seems to me, are two: first, a bone-deep resistance to the idea that there might be anything at all wrong with his or her position; second, an equally deep conviction that anyone who disagrees in any way with that position must be doing so from some combination of ignorance, fear, and ill will rather than from a principled and logical perspective.

Zealotry comes in many forms and can be found on virtually every part of the spectrum on every issue. Politically, we all know left-wing or right-wing zealots—it's even possible to be a middle-of-the-road zealot if you feel that political moderation is the only answer to every issue. Most of us know (and are friends on Facebook with) at least one dietary

This essay was originally published in *Against the Grain* 25, no. 5 (November 2013): 84.

zealot. Hang around long enough in the scholarly communication field, and you're liable to meet zealots who are either for or against print books, e-books, open access, traditional subscription models, copyright, Creative Commons licensing, institutional repositories, and patron-driven acquisition. And Prezi—let's not even talk about Prezi.

It's important not to confuse zealotry with passion or enthusiasm. All of us are passionate about certain issues and pursuits, but most of us are able to keep our enthusiasm at least somewhat under control and in perspective. You may love government documents, but you probably don't turn every meeting you attend into a seminar on how to use government documents better; you may be enthusiastic about patron-driven acquisition, but hopefully you don't shout down anyone who raises concerns about it.

That said, most of us have zealot tendencies to some degree; for almost all of us, there is at least one topic about which we struggle to talk rationally, so great is our passion either for or against it. But, again, most of us are aware of these quirks in ourselves and try to keep them limited and under control. Real zealots have no such self-awareness, which can make their company pretty exhausting—and if you work in close proximity to one, heaven help you.

Most of the time zealotry is pretty easy to spot, which is handy. But sometimes it flies under the radar, which is why I'm offering this brief field guide to some of its symptoms. Here are some rhetorical characteristics and tendencies that can clue you in to the fact that you're probably in the presence of a zealot.

Symptoms of Zealotry

1. A tendency to double down on arguments that don't support the position.
   Zealot: We can't migrate our print journal subscriptions online because not everyone has Internet access.
   You: But far more of our patrons have Internet access than have easy access to our print collection.
   Zealot: Maybe so, but there are still lots of people without Internet access.

2. Unwillingness to acknowledge downsides to the position.
   You: What problems do you foresee if we adopt your proposal?
   Zealot: Well, I can tell you what problems you'll have if we don't.

3. Confusion of "is" with "ought." (When shown that things are not as he wishes they were, the zealot will focus on how things ought to be.)

   You: No one has used Database X in three years, and our budget is very tight. I think it's time to cancel it.

   Zealot: But it's such a great database. People really should be using it more.

   You: We've been actively promoting it for three years, and there's still no demand for it.

   Zealot: We obviously need to promote it harder.

4. Ad hominem and "poisoned well" argumentation.

   Zealot: Why are you giving Mr. X a forum in your publication? He works with an organization that opposes [favored political goal].

   Editor: Our publication has absolutely nothing to do with [favored political goal].

   Zealot: Well, I don't think you should give someone like him a forum at all.

5. Attribution of evil motivations to anyone who disagrees.

   You: I have real concerns about the implications of compulsory CC BY licensing for authors' rights.

   Zealot: Why do you hate openness and sharing?

6. Characterization of all opposition as fear.

   You: I have real concerns about the implications of compulsory CC BY licensing for authors' rights.

   Zealot: Why are you so scared of openness and sharing?

7. A dogged focus on intended consequences, and unwillingness to acknowledge unintended ones.

   You: If Green OA mandates are implemented widely, it's really going to impact revenue streams for society publishers.

   Zealot: No, no—the purpose of OA is not to hurt publishers; it's to make research results accessible to all.

8. Slippery-slope arguments.

   You: I think we should start wearing badges that identify us as library employees, so patrons can tell who works here and is available to help them.

   Zealot: Great. The next thing you know, we're going to have tattooed bar codes on our foreheads.

9. Caricature.

   You: I think we should start wearing badges that identify us as library employees, so patrons can tell who works here and is available to help them.

   Zealot: So you're saying you want to turn the library into Wal-Mart?

10. Every battle is a Glorious Victory, but the war is never won.

    Zealots understand these two principles right down to their bones: First, Glorious Victories are very important because they keep the warriors feeling motivated and encouraged. Second, no matter how many Glorious Victories you achieve, you can never admit that the war is over because doing so tends to cause your warriors to go home (and if you're a professional zealot, the end of the war may very well mean that you've lost your job).

Now, please note: To point out the dangers of zealotry is not to say that every controversial issue has two equally reasonable sides to it, or that every opinion on every issue should be regarded as equally valid. There really are intractable realities that have to be acknowledged if we're going to move forward with our work in a reasonably effective way, and very often those intractable realities favor one opinion more than another. Budgets are limited; some access models serve the most people more effectively than others; spending a dollar on Project X leaves one dollar less to spend on Project Y. Perspectives that don't account for things as they really are can't be given the same weight as those that do.

But it's also true that every position, every solution, and every strategy involves tradeoffs of some kind, and every one features a mix of positive and negative aspects. Even when you have only one feasible choice, that choice will be characterized by both good and bad aspects and will carry with it both positive and negative consequences. An unwillingness to acknowledge and deal constructively with that mix is a hallmark of unconstructive zealotry—and does all of us more harm than good. It's also true that figuring out how "things really are" is not always easy. The number of books on a shelf is a matter of observable reality, and not really susceptible to multiple opinions; the appropriate balance of allocations between books and journals is a judgment call.

Most importantly, when it comes to keeping an eye out for zealotry, each of us should probably start by looking in the mirror and ensuring that we don't see any there. You and I won't, of course—and anyone who suggests we might is an idiot.

18

It's Not about the Workflow

Patron-Centered Practices for
Twenty-First-Century Serialists

ON ITS FACE, the idea of "patron-centered" serials work may not seem to make much sense. After all, serials librarians don't usually have much direct interaction with patrons at all; our work is conducted behind the scenes, and our primary job is to acquire content and make it ready for patrons to use, not to shape the library's public services or to provide those services to patrons directly.

But developments in the information world generally (and in libraries in particular) over the past decade have conspired to blur the boundaries between technical services and public services. It's becoming less and less possible to separate the products we provide (books, journals, databases) from the services that patrons use to gain access to them; increasingly, what libraries provide are direct links to content, not just descriptions of content and directions to the content's physical location. This means that serialists must think more carefully than we once had to about the effects our practices and workflows have on patrons. Where we once concerned ourselves primarily with serving patrons *indirectly* by following standards and setting up predictable, consistent workflows, we now must think in terms of serving them *directly* by being flexible and responsive to their changing needs.

This essay was originally published as "It's Not about the Workflow: Patron-Centered Practices for 21st-Century Serialists" in *Serials Librarian* 51, no. 3–4 (2007): 189–199, and is reprinted by permission. It incorporates a column titled "Four Mantras for the Patron-Centered Technical Services Librarian" from *Against the Grain* 17, no. 4 (September 2005): 86–87.

The most fundamental and significant development in our patrons' information world has been an explosion in the amount of high-quality information that is freely available to them and easily found on the Internet. That explosion has happened within the past fifteen years. Library services that are designed to meet the problem of information scarcity seem irrelevant to today's user, who sees the world as a place of dizzying, kaleidoscopic information abundance—a place where the challenge is to pluck the answer to one's question from a huge pile of readily available information, not one where the answer can be found in only one or two places and must be laboriously sought out. Patrons are bemused when someone suggests that they might have to go physically to the library to find the answer to a question (even in those rare cases where that's actually true). In a particular instance, one might be able to convince a patron that this is so, but for most people, the need to "go to the library" will be seen as an exception to the information-seeking rule.

While we in the library profession do a good job of talking about the importance of looking to the future, embracing change, and so forth, we haven't yet come to terms with the fundamental and radical changes that have taken place in the information economy. While a complete inventory of the present and future impacts of those changes is beyond the scope of this essay, I'll focus here on some specific ways in which we, as serialists, can change the way we think about our departmental practices and workflows and thereby make them more useful to patrons whose lives and research practices have already been deeply impacted by fundamental shifts in the nature of the information world.

Four Mantras

Slogans can be dangerous. Whether they're invoked by politicians or librarians, they tend to short-circuit the critical thought process and reduce complex issues to handy sound bites that make us feel good without bringing us any closer to real solutions to real problems. So I'd prefer not to call the following four phrases "slogans." Instead, I like to think of them as mantras—thoughts that we can chant quietly to ourselves at the beginning of each workday so as to get ourselves into an appropriately patron-centered frame of mind. None of them offers a specific solution to a specific problem; instead, each touches on a facet of patron-centered thinking.[1]

Mantra #1: Our job is not to manage information, but to deliver it. Obviously, managing information is important, and it's a very large part of what we do every day. But it's not the ultimate purpose of our work; our goal is not to have a well-managed collection. We manage our collection well so that our patrons will have easier, faster, and more intuitive access to its content. If we see management of the collection as our goal, our perspective will be library-centered (or, even worse, librarian-centered). If we see delivery of information as our goal, then our perspective will be patron-centered.

Mantra #2: Don't try to think like a good librarian; try to think like a bad patron. As good librarians, we try to do things the way they're supposed to be done. We follow the rules; we make sure that our records are completely accurate and exhaustive; we try multiple search strategies and tailor our searches precisely using carefully thought-out criteria. Our finding tools tend to be designed on the assumption that our patrons will do the same thing. But they don't, and that's why Google has completely eaten our lunch as a discovery tool. Google is designed for people who have never heard of Boolean logic, who have no time to waste on carefully calibrated and adjusted search arguments, who (as the new cliché goes) want to *find* rather than *search*. We can try to reform our patrons, but we won't have much luck; there are too many of them and too few of us, for one thing, and for another, even those we reach are unlikely to change their behavior drastically as a result of our interventions.

Mantra #3: Not everything worth doing is worth doing well (let alone perfectly).[2] Your dad may have been right about most things, but he was wrong about this one. Not everything worth doing is worth doing well—there are things that have to be done but that are not important enough to justify the amount of time and effort it would take to do them perfectly. These should be done quickly and as well as *necessary*, not as well as *possible*. What are those things? The answer will vary from library to library, of course, but the question should be asked about every process in your departmental workflow. And the best way to phrase the question is not "How does this practice make us a better library?" but, rather, "How does this practice benefit our patrons?" Remember that library standards are a tool to be used in the service of patrons, not an ultimate goal to which patron service is a secondary concern.

Mantra #4: You can't eliminate error; you can only prioritize it. All of us have had experiences with people who want to train you and train you and train you until you never make another mistake. These people labor under a dangerous illusion: that it is possible to eliminate mistakes by training. The reality is that mistakes are going to happen, and we have to make rational choices about which ones we'll work harder to prevent and which ones we'll let slide and correct later (if at all). When we pretend to be eliminating error, what we're actually doing is abdicating the responsibility to prioritize it; we're letting chance or organizational inertia determine where the mistakes will be made and left uncorrected. No library has enough supervisory staff to monitor every output of every employee every day. So what we have to do is decide which errors are most likely to have a negative impact on patron service, put the most emphasis on preventing and correcting those, and settle for less perfection in less important areas. That doesn't mean letting chaos reign in those areas, but acknowledging that with limited staff time the less important processes simply have to get less oversight than the more important ones.

What Do Patron-Centered Workflows Look Like?

Because different libraries serve different types of patrons with different types of needs, there is no single set of workflows that will provide equally good patron service in all libraries. But patron-centered workflows will all have certain identifiable characteristics. Four particularly important ones are:

A high level of efficiency. Every once in a while, I hear a librarian talk about "celebrating inefficiency," and a little part of me dies. Let's be clear about one thing: as professional librarians, we do not celebrate inefficiency. Inefficiency means using resources badly; specifically, it means using more of a resource (time, money, energy) than is necessary to accomplish the desired task. Libraries notoriously never have enough time or money, and our stores of human energy are limited as well. This means that we have a responsibility to marshal our limited resources rationally and wisely. And, yes, this does mean always seeking "the most bang for our buck"—where "bang" means "patron service" and "buck" means "a unit of money, time, or energy."

A focus on speed-to-stacks. The patron-centered librarian will design workflows that make library materials (in all formats) available as quickly as possible to patrons. This doesn't mean handling processes with reckless speed, of course, but the patron-centered library will avoid assuming that perfect accuracy or thoroughness is always worth what it costs in promptness. There's a very big difference between saying to ourselves, "We have to do this slowly in order to serve our patrons well" and saying, "We have to do this slowly or else we'll make a mistake." Not all mistakes are equally important. For example, it's important to make sure that the book we've received is one for which we have a standing order. On the other hand, is it worth it to make patrons wait while we measure the book's standing height in centimeters (even if taking that measurement "takes only a few seconds")?

Cost-effectiveness. Cost-effectiveness is closely related to efficiency, but it's not quite the same thing. More than just avoiding waste, it means always weighing costs against benefits when making decisions about what work is to be done and boldly (or tremulously, if need be) making cuts and changes when benefits aren't sufficient to justify costs. Remember that costs aren't always measured in dollars; staff time and energy are limited resources as well and therefore have to be budgeted. If our investments of time and energy aren't bringing back solid benefits to our patrons, then we need to rethink the way we're using those resources.

Designed with patrons, not librarians, in mind. It's a cruel truth, but a truth nonetheless, that the library does not exist to provide employment for us. Librarians (like collections) are a means to an end, and the end is the provision of information services to patrons. Remember Mantra #2: we need to put ourselves in the shoes of patrons who don't know what they're doing and are too busy or embarrassed to ask for help. So when, for example, you analyze the features of an online search interface, the question to ask yourself is not "Does this interface provide all the options that we, as good librarians, think it should?" but, rather, "How helpful will this interface be to a patron who has no idea what he's doing and isn't inclined to ask for help?" When organizing a serials workflow, the patron-centered librarian asks first how quickly and easily her patrons should be able to get access to received materials, and then works backward from that goal to her back-office practices. (The librarian-centered librarian, on the other hand, starts with a set of preferred back-office practices and allows them to define limits on patron service.)

Questions We Need to Ask about Our Current Workflows

Not every patron-centered library will have the same policies and practices, of course. If all of them did, they wouldn't be patron-centered, since different libraries serve different kinds of patrons with sometimes widely varying sets of needs. But there are certain questions that all such libraries will ask themselves, and though the answers to those questions will vary, the principles that lie behind them are the same. These include:

Are we putting work on our patrons that the library staff could reasonably do instead? When evaluating a service, stop yourself from saying things like, "Yes, this interface is a pain to use, but our patrons are more than capable of filling out a simple online form." The librarian-centered librarian asks, "Is this requirement something that our patrons ought to be able to handle?" whereas the patron-centered librarian asks, "Is there a reasonable way to remove this particular roadblock from my patrons' path?"

Are we delaying the end result unnecessarily? This question is related to the "speed-to-stacks" issue. Remember that every step in a workflow comes at a cost. One of the costs is delay; the more time you spend processing materials, the less quickly those materials will be made available to your patrons. The patron-centered librarian makes it a point to review his workflows regularly, looking critically at each step and asking whether its cost is justified in terms of patron benefit. (In most cases, the answer will be yes, because most workflows are set up more or less rationally, but it's important to keep asking the question. Otherwise, workflows harden and turn into traditions that no one questions.)

Am I putting professional standards ahead of improved service? Remember that professional standards are not rules written on stone tablets by the finger of Deity. They are criteria that librarians set for themselves, and they may or may not always lead to the best possible service for our patrons. We should never hesitate to break with professional norms and standards if doing so will provide better service to our patrons. None of this is to say that professional standards are bad, of course; it's only to say that they should be kept in their place. They're good to the exact degree that they result in better service to library patrons.

Examples of Workflows That May Degrade Service

Most of our serials workflows were originally designed to manage printed materials. In a world in which scholarly journals have moved decisively (if not quite universally) online, we need to stop and think about whether our print-based practices still make sense. Four practices that are particularly strong candidates for radical change are:

Routine claiming. Steven D. Zink and I have made a detailed case for the elimination of routine check-in and claiming elsewhere, but I'll repeat here one small piece of our argument concerning the standard practice of claiming.[3] To get an idea of the usefulness of routine claiming, try this thought experiment: Imagine all the journal issues that are expected to arrive in your library in a given year. Now subtract from that number all the issues that arrive on time (or close enough to on time that you wouldn't normally claim them). We generally assume that the number left over is the number of issues on which our claiming practices have a beneficial impact. But this isn't so, because a significant number of the issues we claim would have arrived even if we hadn't claimed them; they are late but will arrive eventually. That number must be subtracted from the previous total, since claiming has no meaningful effect on those issues. But there's another problem: from the number that now remains, we must also subtract the issues that will never arrive regardless of how many times we claim them. The number that is now left is the number of journal issues on which routine claiming activity actually has a beneficial impact. However, there's one more hitch, and that lies in the fact that routine claiming doesn't only generate solutions; it also generates problems, mainly in the form of duplicate issues. The question that a conscientious serialist should ask himself is whether that final number of positively affected issues is great enough to justify both the cost of the work involved in claiming and the cost of the problems caused by claiming. The answer may be yes, but the question needs to be asked.

Binding. In many cases, routine binding of older journal issues is a matter of giving expensive and labor-intensive protection to materials that require little or no protection at all—because they'll get little, if any, use in the future. A patron-centered librarian will stop and think about whether the time and money invested in traditional binding could be better spent on other activities that provide a better return in terms of patron service. Cheaper and less time-intensive alternatives do exist; one such is explored in the article cited above.

Authority work. While some kinds of authority work (such as for author names) are clearly essential to making content available to our users, other kinds may be less so. At the University of Nevada, Reno, we decided to stop doing subject authority work because our staff was small and because it was clear that very few patrons ever used subject headings for searching. This isn't to say that subject authority work has no value—only that given the hard reality of a small staff and a huge number of new tasks that have to be accomplished, we had to make difficult decisions about which valuable tasks would be kept and which would be abandoned. Some of our new tasks (such as updating lists of available online journals) had much more impact on patron service than some of our old ones (such as subject authority work), so we decided to give them a higher priority in the investment of our scarce staff time.

Unnecessary record customization. Here's another thought experiment, this one for serials catalogers: If you were to accept OCLC member copy without editing it, how many records could you add to your catalog in a four-hour period? Now, if you carefully review and edit those records before adding them to your catalog, by how many will that number be reduced? The gap between those numbers represents the benefit of not editing OCLC member records. There's a cost as well, of course: the unedited records may not do as good a job of connecting your patrons with your collection as edited ones would have. So you need to ask yourselves another question: "Which will benefit our patrons more, the larger number of unedited records or the smaller number of edited ones?" Different libraries may answer that question in different ways, but, again, what is essential is asking this particular (patron-centered) question, rather than the (librarian-centered) question that is more typically (if tacitly) asked: "How can we make these records as perfect as possible?"

Characteristics of Workflows That Serve Patrons Well

No single workflow will serve every patron equally well, of course. Unfortunately, we don't have the capacity to provide perfect service to every patron. Our only option is to do our best to serve as many patrons as possible as perfectly as we can. With this inevitable compromise in mind, let me close by suggesting three characteristics of workflows that tend to provide the best possible service to as many patrons as possible.

Patron-centered workflows will tend to place a higher priority on online access than on print access. It's common to hear librarians say that "online isn't necessarily better than print." But this is hogwash. When it comes to doing research using journal content, online access is dramatically better than print access in just about every way imaginable. (Not everything is available online, of course, but that just means that in some cases we have to settle for an inferior research medium; it doesn't mean that online isn't better.) Online allows users to search the full text of research materials, to use the content wherever they are and whenever they want, to save or print all or some of the relevant text as they see fit—the benefits just go on and on and shouldn't require much more elaboration. The point here is that patron-centered workflows will be built around the recognition that for research journals, online really is better than print. Requests for new subscriptions to print journals will be sent back unless the requestor can demonstrate that online isn't available (or that print is needed for some specific reason); management of online resources will take precedence over management of print ones; online access problems will be given a higher priority over questions that arise from print subscriptions. Exceptions to those rules will arise, but they'll be determined by the needs of patrons—not by appeals to standard practice or tradition.

Patron-centered workflows will tend to be automated. Products like Serials Solutions and the various emerging electronic resource management systems (such as the one currently offered by Innovative Interfaces, Inc.) offer excellent opportunities to automate what would otherwise be inefficient, labor-intensive, and error-prone manual processes. These products aren't perfect, of course, but neither are the manual processes that they replace. Remember, again, that we don't have the option of eliminating error; we can only reduce it and prioritize it. The threat of imperfection is never a sufficient reason to rule out automating procedures that can be automated, although it's important to investigate carefully the particular types of errors that are likely to arise and be certain that patrons really are likely to realize a net benefit from the change.

Patron-centered workflows will tend to be tolerant of minor error. A workflow that involves constant checking to catch and resolve all errors is one that will end up serving patrons badly. A patron-centered workflow will prioritize error-correcting processes by importance, investing time in the resolution of serious errors ("serious" meaning "likely to have a serious impact on patron service") and allowing inconsequential errors to slip through. The definitions of "serious" and "inconsequential" will vary from library to library, of course, depending on the amount of staff available to catch and fix errors, the types of research materials involved, the kinds of patrons served by the library, etc.

Conclusion

There are those who believe that to consciously adopt a patron-centered mind-set is to treat ourselves and our libraries as businesses that kowtow to the customer's every whim, flattering him that he's always right and bending over backward to make his interaction with the business as easy and pleasant as possible. This goes against our grain. Instead of arguing over fine distinctions between the "customer service" mind-set and the "patron-centered" mind-set, let me simply suggest that it may be time for us to swallow our pride. Libraries, especially academic ones, exist to help patrons do their scholarly work. Patrons have alternatives to libraries that did not exist until very recently. If we want to be useful to those we are here to serve, then we have to deal with the fact that we are now in a competitive situation. If our resources and services are less attractive to researchers than the growing array of alternatives, then they will stop using our resources and services. We may console ourselves by saying that our resources are generally better than the free, easy-to-use alternatives. But those alternatives are getting better, more comprehensive, and more easy to use every day. Can we say the same for our services?

NOTES

1. This section of the essay was previously published, in different form, in the September 2005 issue of *Against the Grain* as an entry in my column "IMHBCO (In My Humble But Correct Opinion)." The piece was titled "Four Mantras for the Patron-Centered Technical Services Librarian."
2. For further discussion of this concept, see essay 13 in this volume.
3. Rick Anderson and Steven D. Zink, "Implementing the Unthinkable: The Demise of Periodical Check-In at the University of Nevada," *Library Collections, Acquisitions, and Technical Services* 27 (2003): 61–71.

19

Can't Buy Us Love

The Declining Importance of Library Books and the Rising Importance of Special Collections

RESEARCH LIBRARIES throughout North America are experiencing a massive decline in the use of their general collections—their large and comprehensive collections of printed books and journal volumes purchased in the commercial marketplace.[1] This decline is the inevitable outcome of the radical shift in scholarly publishing from an analog and print-based model to a digital and networked one. In this environment, it is no longer obvious that it makes sense for research libraries to continue their traditional practice of creating, housing, and maintaining such collections. In this essay, I will propose that we shift our focus from the collection of what we might call "commodity" documents (especially in physical formats) to another activity in which we have also been engaging for many centuries: the gathering and curating of rare and unique documents, including primary-source materials.

The Radical Shift Is Not the Format Shift

For centuries, readers and researchers have relied on academic libraries to provide them with access to books that are sold (or access to which is sold) in the commercial marketplace. Patrons relied on libraries to solve what were essentially problems of market inefficiency: Books were expensive physical objects that cost a lot to create, move, orga-

This essay was originally published as an ITHAKA S+R Briefing Paper, August 1, 2013.

nize, and maintain. Since books were expensive, no one could buy all the books he or she needed, and since they were bulky and heavy and fragile and prone to loss, the cost of housing and caring for large collections of books was prohibitive even if the cost of buying them was not. By pooling institutional resources, research libraries made access to these expensive resources available, on a shared basis, to all in their host institutions and undertook their housing and preservation as well.

The same thing has remained true even after scholarly communication moved largely out of the physical and analog environment and into a networked and digital environment: access to online journals (which are used far more heavily than monographs, especially printed monographs, in research libraries) and e-books remains very expensive, even though the costs of processing and "housing" online documents are dramatically lower. This has meant that throughout much of the 1990s and early 2000s, the role of the research library as a broker (buying access on behalf of a large community of users), a curator (ensuring that access endures), and an organizer (making resources easier to find and use) remained important even as the acquisition and housing of research content moved substantially into a virtual environment.

However, during the past two decades, the networked digital environment has done more than just become the default locus of scholarly communication. It has done three other things as well.

1. It has *made the market for "commodity" books much more efficient*, driving the price of books down. By "price," I do not mean average list price—which has remained relatively stable over time—but rather the actual amount of money typically paid for a copy of a book.[2] In the past, if one wanted to buy a book, the cheapest option available was the cheapest local option: if the lowest price in a nearby bookstore was $20, that was the best deal most buyers could hope for. With the advent of such Internet-based outlets as Amazon Marketplace and Bookfinder. com, however, every home with an Internet connection has direct access to the holdings of thousands and thousands of bookstores around the world, and the likelihood of finding a remaindered or used copy—often at a price of literally pennies, plus a few dollars in shipping—is very high. Prior to 1995, a library had to be careful not to lose its 1975 printing of, say, Steinbeck's *East of Eden* and had to take good care of that copy lest it fall to pieces from decay or use. In 2013, the loss of the library's physical copy of a commodity book has little, if any, impact on its patrons'

access to that book. As of this writing, replacement copies of *East of Eden* can be had from more than a hundred online booksellers at a cost of one dollar or less, plus shipping. This means not only that the library can afford to take less scrupulous care of its existing copy but also—and much more importantly—that the library's patrons simply no longer depend on the library for access to that book in the way they once did.

2. The new information environment has *greatly reduced the cost of information distribution,* making it much easier for scholars to share documents (such as articles that they or others have written) with one another. New technology has also made it possible to digitize and make publicly available an enormous corpus of public-domain books—physical copies of which still cost money in the commercial marketplace, and which of course also cost money to house and care for. Online aggregations like Google Books and the Hathi Trust, by putting digital copies of public-domain titles into a publicly available online database, have effectively obviated the need for most libraries to hold physical copies of those books. By joining Hathi Trust in 2010 and thus gaining full-text access (along with full download rights) to that collection's 3.3 million public-domain books, the research library in which I work effectively doubled the size of its book collection—and at a trivial cost. Costs of distribution should not be confused with costs of publication; however, the ease with which documents may now be distributed after (or before) publication means that scholars no longer rely on libraries for access to those documents in the way they once did. Professors whose libraries do not subscribe to the journal containing a needed article would once have argued strenuously for a subscription or requested a copy via interlibrary loan; today, they are just as likely to contact the article's author directly and request a copy by e-mail, in many cases receiving a positive response within hours or even minutes. This is admittedly not a terribly efficient way to get access to journal articles, and the pressure on libraries to maintain strong subscription lists remains great. But the fact that such an informal acquisition network now exists leads to the third impact that a pervasively networked digital information environment has had on the scholarly communication system.

3. It has made possible the *open-access (OA) movement*, which could never have existed in a print-based information environment. The movement's success to this point has relied, in part, on the widely held perception that the digital environment has virtually eliminated publication costs, in part on assertions about what the public pays for when it funds scientific research, and in part on the undeniable fact that once a document has been placed on the network, the cost of creating and distributing an additional copy of that document falls to virtually nothing. The degree to which institutional or governmental OA policies, combined with publishers' adoption of author-pays OA models, will succeed at turning what were once commodity documents into effectively public property remains to be seen, but the movement's success has been considerable so far and it continues to grow.

What makes these three developments significant for the future of libraries is that, together, they point to a single, potentially transformative reality.

Focusing on the Wrong Shift

When, in the 1990s, it became clear that the scholarly communication system was moving almost entirely out of the print realm and onto a worldwide digital network, we in libraries immediately began dealing with this development as a format shift: whereas we had been brokers, curators, and organizers of print collections, we now prepared ourselves to become brokers, curators, and organizers of online collections. We focused on what this shift would mean for our workflows, for patron access, for privacy, for preservation, and for our traditional discovery tools. Much ink was spilled and many trees killed as we argued about how best to address and adjust to these changes—but, in general, I believe we have made that adjustment quite well. The typical research library does an admirable job of making enormous amounts of relevant and high-quality information in a variety of formats available with reasonable ease to its patrons and has created a new superstructure of services designed to ensure reasonable permanence of access where such is needed. We have established buying consortia to give our budgets extra leverage and to create economies of scale and have built tools to make management of online resources more effective and more cost-efficient. Our response to the print-to-online shift has not been perfect, but we have generally been successful at turning ourselves substantially from brokers, curators, and organizers of print materials into brokers, curators, and organizers of online digital materials.

However, during these past two decades of radical change and energetic response, I believe we have missed a much more important shift, one that poses a more direct and existential threat than the one posed by the move from print to online. We have failed to prepare for the emergence of a reality in which our very role as brokers, curators, and organizers has itself been fundamentally undermined.

In other words, the gap that should most concern us in research libraries today is not the one that lies between *physical and online documents*, but the one that lies between *commodity and non-commodity documents*. The library's important role as a broker arose largely because of the many inherent inefficiencies of a print-based information marketplace. Today's more efficient online marketplace features much lower prices and much lower barriers to personal collection-building, a pervasive full-text searching capability that makes traditional cataloging less obviously necessary, and widely distributed storage and access points that undermine traditional approaches to preservation and curation. This new reality affects commodity documents no matter the format, though its impact is most obvious in the book marketplace—particularly the market for trade books that are produced in large print runs. (It is less the case in the journal economy, where there is no appreciable secondary market, and therefore quickly rising subscription prices pose a much higher barrier to individual access.) The bottom line is that libraries are no longer needed in the way they once were to provide access to documents that are available in the commercial marketplace.

The Janus-Faced Library

If the library's roles as a broker, curator, and organizer of commodity documents are fading, what significant roles remain?

Virtually every academic library is really two very different organizations housed in a single building and united by an artificial administrative connection. The first library, the one everyone sees, is that which manages a collection of commodity documents, in both print and online formats. The library imposes less control on this collection, allowing its contents to be used without supervision; this is because the materials in the general collection tend not to be unique or even rare and can usually be repaired or replaced without any loss of value to the patron. The second is the library that we typically call "special collections." Materials in special collections are typically much more tightly controlled because they are not easily replaced and physical repair might significantly reduce their value. A library that acquires a copy of Andreas Cellarius's seventeenth-century *Harmonia Macrocosmica* is not doing so because that document will provide the astronomy faculty good information about the solar system, or even to show what seventeenth-century scientists believed about the solar system (which could be accomplished much more cheaply and conveniently with a transcription or a facsimile copy). It is doing so in order to preserve and provide carefully controlled access to a beautiful and rare document, the value of which may have as much to do with illuminating the history of binding and printing as the history of science.

Thus, whereas the main library buys documents primarily because of their *curricular relevance and instrumental value*, special collections is often more interested in documents as *artifacts that are valuable in and of themselves*, independent of the immediate relevance or utility of the words and ideas they contain—documents that, in a great many cases, are rare or fragile enough to be in serious danger of loss without special care. Thus, a mass-market 1975 printing of *East of Eden* will be shelved in a public area of the library, where patrons may take it down and peruse it at will and even take it home with the promise eventually to return it; if the book falls apart, it will likely not be repaired but, rather, replaced—perhaps even with a different edition. In the circulating collection, the content matters much more than the container. Special collections, on the other hand, is more likely to hold a signed first edition of that same book, which will be made available for use by patrons only under supervision and in a tightly controlled environment. Under no circumstances will a patron be allowed to remove that item from the library. If it is damaged, replacement would be extremely difficult and repair costly; in the case of unique materials, replacement would be simply impossible. In special collections the content matters, but the container often matters more.

The rare and unique materials held by special collections are, in other words, not commodity documents. While they may be bought and sold in a marketplace, it is a highly specialized marketplace with a unique structure and unique rules. It is not Amazon, and most members of the general public do not have ready access to it. In quite a few cases, in fact, the materials held by a research library's special collections are not purchased by the library at all but are given to the library by donors working outside the commercial marketplace entirely.

The Distinction That Will Shape Our Future

It is the opportunities inherent in this distinction—the distinction between commodity documents and non-commodity documents—that I believe will bear heavily on the future utility and health of the academic research library. The print/online dichotomy is no longer a terribly meaningful one, and indeed it may have been a red herring from the start, mere camouflage for the real shift that was happening, which was a dramatic increase in the efficiency of the marketplace for commodity documents. As the efficiency of that marketplace increases, and as unassisted discovery of those documents continues to become easier and easier, many of the academic library's traditional roles are moving to the margins of the research experience. In short, very few academic patrons truly rely on their library to buy, process, describe, and preserve a 1975 printing of *East of Eden*. However, if that library's special collections owns a handwritten poem by a ninth-century Arab poet, or a handwritten journal from a Civil War combatant, and fails to curate that item, the entire world (not just the library's local constituency) suffers—particularly in situations where the library is holding a collection on behalf of a community that lacks a strong archiving or publishing infrastructure of its own.

What, then, does curating such a document entail? In the past, it meant keeping the document in a tightly controlled protective environment and drastically restricting access to it. In today's environment, it means doing the same—but much, much more as well.

What the world needs research libraries to do now—and this need is both powerful and growing—is provide broad and easy access to the intellectual content of rare and unique non-commodity documents that would otherwise remain unfindable and unusable. This means:

1. *Acquiring them.* Rare and unique documents held by private collectors, or languishing unknown in archives and basements, do the world of scholarship very little good. Libraries have money to spend on documents and need to direct more of that money away from the purchase of commodity documents that are already relatively freely and easily available to the public and toward the acquisition of documents that, unless they are held by libraries, will not be made available to scholars in any meaningful way.
2. *Digitizing them.* A library that owns a rare or unique book and simply keeps it locked up is doing the world no greater service than a private collector who does the same. While physical

access will generally have to be restricted in order to preserve the document, access to the *words, ideas, and images* contained in the document can and should be made available as widely as possible. This can be done most effectively by creating high-resolution images of those contents and disseminating the images online.

3. *Making them discoverable.* Access is not only limited by format, policy, and practice; it is also limited by findability. What makes documents findable is good metadata (including, as needed, transcription and/or translation), organized and optimized to expose itself promiscuously to popular search engines. A document that cannot be found is, for all intents and purposes, nonexistent.

Uniqueness and Mission

There is a potentially serious barrier for any library that wishes to move aggressively in the direction I have described; that barrier is the mission of its host institution. For a major research library to suddenly and unilaterally redirect, say, 50 percent of its collections budget to the acquisition and processing of rare and unique materials would be both irresponsible and unwise. We must bear in mind that while such materials will, in many cases, offer tremendous value to the wider world of scholarship, and while in some cases it may be possible (and even tremendously beneficial) to incorporate those materials into the local curriculum, rare and unique documents may not always provide direct support to the most centrally important mission elements and strategic directions of any individual library's host institution.

This implies several important realities:

1. Every research library must *strike the right balance* between benefiting the larger world of scholarship and supporting its institution's specific teaching and learning and research goals. If it fails to do so, it will lose the support of its host—and rightly so. Furthermore, what constitutes the right balance should (and, in the long run, will) be determined by the host institution, not by the library.

2. Most of the people served by a research library spend little or no time thinking about the difference between commodity and non-commodity documents and may be only peripherally aware of the tremendous changes that have taken place in the scholarly communication economy. In order to gain support for some

degree of shift in priorities away from traditional commodity documents and toward non-commodity ones, librarians will have to *explain clearly, concisely, and compellingly* why such a shift makes sense and how it will be beneficial in terms of both local and broader public good. Support for the shift will be determined by a combination of high-level institutional buy-in and general acceptance of the explanation by the library's on-the-ground patron constituency.

3. For most libraries, the shift will have to be gradual. Key to success will be enacting the shift in a *steady, realistic, and wholly transparent* manner. The appropriate speed and trajectory of the shift will vary from library to library and will have to be determined in consultation with institutional administrators. At all points, it will have to be enacted in an open and transparent way.

The qualifying language in each of the above points is absolutely essential. It is a hard truth, but true nevertheless, that an academic library does not (and should not) define its own role on campus. It can (and should) actively contribute to the shaping of its role, and library leaders absolutely must both develop and promulgate an expansive and ambitious vision. But veto power lies with the leadership of the host institution. The academic library exists to move the university forward, not vice versa.[3] Library leaders who lose sight of this fundamental fact will eventually lose their jobs.

An Opportunity to Sidestep the Scholarly Communication Wars

There is an ancillary but significant benefit to shifting the focus from commodity to non-commodity documents. The politics and economics of scholarly communication are increasingly fraught. Publishers (both for-profit and not-for-profit) working in the commercial marketplace defend their revenue streams; libraries fight to keep prices down; authors submit their manuscripts to the publications most likely to help them secure prestige and tenure while (for the most part) trying to stay out of the skirmishes constantly breaking out between publishers and libraries; and readers either get access to scholarly publications or do not, depending on their institutional affiliations or their personal buying power.

Over the past two decades, librarians have grown increasingly frustrated with the existing scholarly communication system, calling on one another to create an alternative, noncommercial structure based in the academy rather than in the marketplace, and calling on authors to stop supporting the old one.[4] But the traditional system exerts a very powerful gravity—so powerful, in fact, that even when OA models have taken hold and begun to flourish, they have generally been absorbed into the traditional system rather than subverting it. The so-called Gold OA model[5] (the one that has been willingly adopted by many STM publishers and functionally enshrined in national policy thanks to the UK's Finch Report[6]) does not undermine the old system so much as enrich it, and while it does result in better access for readers, it also shifts costs to funding agencies and research budgets—and thus away from the support of research itself. Whether one sees this as a good thing or a bad thing on balance depends on one's perspective and goals. Those who were hoping that OA would put commercial science publishers out of business can only be disappointed by such developments, whereas those for whom expanded access is most important have reason to be happy about them.

But a shift in focus from the brokerage of commodity documents to the gathering, processing, management, and wide distribution of non-commodity documents allows us to sidestep the whole open-access-versus toll-access controversy, at least where such documents are concerned. Non-commodity documents are, by definition, not for sale—or at least not in the same way that commodity documents are. A library that shifts a portion of its budget and staff time in the direction of making noncommercial documents more findable and accessible is neither undermining the existing scholarly communication system (except to the extent that it pulls collections money away from commercial purchases) nor supporting it. Instead, it is contributing to a separate system, *one that feeds the scholarly conversation without exerting control over it*; the non-commodity information environment supports scholars without either restricting access to the documents (as the toll-access commodity model does) or constraining authors' publication options (as OA mandates do).

The Situation in One Large Research Library

Allow me to close with an illustration.

The research library in which I work, at the University of Utah, holds in its special collections a number of handwritten diaries produced by nineteenth-century pioneers who came west on the Overland Trail. These documents are unique and fragile and therefore not suitable for circulation or lending, and physical access to them can be granted to researchers only under tightly controlled conditions. They are hand-written in often hard-to-read script and therefore need transcription in order to make their texts machine-readable and electronically search-able. In addition to full-text transcription, making them discoverable by researchers will also require accurate and reasonably comprehensive metadata, including reliable authority records that will ensure they are grouped with similar or related items in search results.

We do not know exactly how many of these diaries we have in our special collections because they are distributed among multiple dona-tions and subcollections that have yet to be fully registered at even the box level, let alone cataloged at the item level. Given the relatively small staff allocated to special collections, it will likely be many years before these diaries are all found and processed—and by that point, many other rare and unique documents will have joined the queue. These diaries represent an incredibly rich and potentially useful set of research materials, and they are only a tiny drop in the enormous bucket of rare and unique documents our library owns. Most of these are virtually unfindable and effectively unusable, because the focus of our library has always been, like that of most libraries, on the gath-ering, organization, and management of commodity documents. Fur-thermore, our library is, in all of these ways, typical of large research libraries throughout the United States—which means that our special collections in their entirety represent only one drop in the much larger bucket of special collections that currently languish, undigitized, unde-scribed, unfindable, and inaccessible in similar libraries throughout our country and the world.

Our library's main, public collection, on the other hand, includes sev-eral million printed commodity books. None of these books is unique and very few are even rare; if lost or damaged, they can virtually all be replaced, generally quite cheaply. A significant portion of them now exists in online versions that are freely available to the public, both for online reading and for downloading in full text.[7] Metadata has already been assigned to these books and, in the vast majority of cases, had already been assigned to them even before we purchased and processed them ourselves. A small and fast-shrinking number of these books is checked out or even consulted by students and faculty in any given year, and yet their acquisition and management absorbs roughly 25 percent of our library's total fund of staff time and they occupy a similar share of the library's increasingly crowded floor space.

Directions for the (Near) Future

Does access to commodity documents matter in a research library? Of course it does. I want to be very clear that I am not advocating that research libraries abandon the brokerage and management of these documents. I am, however, suggesting that research libraries devote a greater percentage of budget and staff time than we hitherto have to the management and dissemination of those rare and unique documents that each of us owns, that no one but the holder can make available to the world, that have the potential greatly to enrich the world of scholarship, and that can be made available outside of the commercial marketplace without damage to any participant in the scholarly communication system. Importantly, I am also urging that each of us make this shift in consultation with our local stakeholders and in harmony with the missions of our host institutions.

One final point: as we begin to move in this direction, it is imperative that we avoid confusing uniqueness with value. The goal of the shift I am describing is not to make the library or its offerings "more unique." Uniqueness may be an important characteristic of a valuable collection, but it has little bearing on value in and of itself. (Given a pen and paper, any one of us could create a perfectly unique but utterly worthless document at a moment's notice.) The goal is to enrich the scholarly environment with useful books and other documents that would otherwise remain hidden from scholars and students, and to shift our focus from resources and activities that make relatively little contribution to that environment to those that will have the greatest enriching effect upon it.

NOTES

1. Rick Anderson, "Print on the Margins: Circulation Trends in Major Research Libraries," *Library Journal* 136 (2011): 38–39.
2. Brent Cox, "How Much More Do Books Cost Today?," *The Awl* (weblog), December 21, 2011, www.theawl.com/2011/12/how-much-more-do-books-cost-today.
3. For further discussion of this principle, see essays 10 and 22 in this volume.
4. The Harvard Library, "Faculty Advisory Council Memorandum on Journal Pricing" (Harvard University, April 17, 2012), http://bit.ly/1PO5qcy.
5. *Wikipedia*, "Open Access," https://en.wikipedia.org/wiki/Open_access.

6.   Research Information Network, "Finch Report" (March 19, 2013), www.researchinfonet.org/publish/finch/.
7.   HathiTrust Digital Library, "HathiTrust Dates—Public Domain," www.hathitrust.org/visualizations_dates_pd.

20

On Knowing the Value of Everything and the Price of Nothing

THERE'S AN OLD APHORISM that says, "A cynic is a man who knows the price of everything and the value of nothing." It's a fair point: knowing what something costs in the marketplace is all well and good, but it doesn't necessarily tell you much about what that thing is "really worth" in any deeper sense. It may cost a baseball team $2 million annually to employ a great player, for example, but is the player's labor really "worth" that much? The market price for a 2007 Bentley Continental GT is around $190,000. Is any car actually worth that much money?

A cynic will snort at the very question: "Hey, if a sucker is willing to pay $190,000 for a car, then that's what the car is worth." But those of us who are less dismissive of morals-and-values questions may be inclined to give the issue a bit more thought. What's a car "really" worth? Its primary value lies in its ability to take you, with reasonable comfort, safety, and speed, from one place to another. A used Chevy Aveo fulfills those basic functions just as well as a Bentley does, and for $180,000 less. What you get if you buy a Bentley instead of an Aveo is a modicum of additional comfort and safety and a great deal of additional prestige. So the real question is whether the prestige conferred on a Bentley driver is worth $180,000. Again, the cynic will say that prestige is worth whatever it can be sold for. You and I, not being cynics, might think about all the people who could be fed, clothed, and educated for $180,000 and conclude that, morally speaking, a Bentley is not worth the price.

This essay was originally published in *Against the Grain* 18, no. 6 (December–January 2006–2007): 44–45.

But before we start congratulating ourselves on our morality and lack of cynicism, we may want to pause for a moment and think about how the aphorism applies in our libraries. Are there things for which we pay a price that is far out of proportion to their value? Or, to put it another way, are we ever guilty of wasting time and money (neither of which is ours to waste) on practices simply because they're "valuable," without considering whether there's a reasonable balance between what they're worth and what they cost?

In libraries, where we recognize a responsibility to serve not only the needs of the majority but also those of often underserved minorities, we tend naturally to think in terms of "just-in-case" scenarios: we need to buy a particular book, this logic goes, not necessarily because we think it will *certainly* be useful to *many* people *now*, but because there's a chance that it *may* be of use to *someone someday*. Similarly, we try to provide for future situations that may not be terribly likely, but that could take place in the future: we send paperbacks out for expensive commercial binding, not because there's any real reason to anticipate heavy use of them, but because they could be damaged if they *were* used heavily; or we carefully track and register changes in a journal's publication patterns because if our catalog fails to reflect the fact that the pattern has changed from quarterly to semiannual, then . . . well . . . something terrible might happen. (Not sure what it is, but something.) Anyway, my point is that many of us exhibit a real inclination to think that as long as we can establish that a practice has value, then the conversation is over: we must do it because it's valuable, or potentially valuable, regardless of what it costs—and anyone who suggests that the practice is too expensive is a cynic who thinks only in terms of the bottom line.

Obviously, though, we can't afford to do everything that's valuable. So, really, we have two choices:

Choice A: Continue doing those valuable things that we've always done, while letting other and potentially more valuable practices wait in the wings.

Choice B: Look at all the options available to us—all the familiar practices plus all the new and/or different options—and choose to do those things that are most valuable first and those things that are less valuable only as time permits.

Choice A allows us to continue doing things that we're good at and that we're comfortable doing; it also entails little risk of upsetting patrons with dramatic changes to our content and services. On the downside, by placing a premium on continuity instead of efficiency and value, it virtually ensures that our services will never improve significantly. On the upside, Choice B puts old and new practices on an equal footing and leads us to judge all practices based on the value they offer rather than letting existing practices stay in place by virtue of inertia. On the downside, it's more work for us.

As professionals, I think it should be clear to us that Choice B is the better of the two. It's not our job to keep doing what's been done in the past, nor is it our job to chuck what's been done in the past and do something different. It's our job to evaluate the available options and pick the ones that will serve our patrons best, while trying to keep our own preferences, prejudices, and comfort out of the equation.

So how does this type of thinking translate into actual, everyday library work? Obviously, it should lead us to think critically about everything we do. Does routine claiming for late journal issues provide value? Of course it does. Is there value in subject authority work, and binding, and bibliographic instruction, and in traditional forms of collection development? Absolutely. But since we have limited—sometimes severely limited—resources, and therefore can't do everything that's valuable, our conversations about workflows, practices, and services have to go beyond the question of what is and isn't valuable. The question that we have to ask ourselves—urgently, dispassionately, and constantly—is whether the things we're doing are the *most* valuable things that we could be doing with the limited amount of time and money available to us. But this begs another question: How will we define value?

I suggest that we do so primarily in terms of patron service. What we do in the library is mainly about bringing patrons together with the information they need. Our purpose isn't to build great collections, nor is it to teach research skills, nor is it to build efficient acquisitions workflows. Those are all things that we do in the service of our primary purpose, which is to get information to patrons. These are not *intrinsically* valuable activities that should be preserved because they're what a good library does; they are *instrumentally* valuable activities that should be preserved only to the extent that they help us toward the goal of connecting people with desired information. We've got to be ready to replace those activities, and any others, with different activities if the different ones will better help patrons get the information they want.

All this is well and good in theory, but what might such decision-making look like in the real world? The Library of Congress exhibited this kind of hardheaded, rational thinking recently when it decided to abandon the creation of series authority records for newly cataloged titles. How did it justify that decision, which enraged many librarians? In a memo dated April 20, 2006, LC explained itself concisely: "We recognize that there are . . . some adverse impacts" (translation: series authority work is valuable), "but they are mitigated when the gains in processing time are considered" (translation: given competing priorities and a limited staff, other needs are more urgent than this one).[1]

Now, LC's thinking may have been sound, but was its decision the best one? From outside the institution, it's difficult to say. Those on the outside, who make use of LC's authority records (and whose patrons theoretically benefit from them), see the adverse effects of LC's decision but can't easily see the upside. What will LC now be able to do that it couldn't before, when its staff was spending time on series authority records? Are the new activities more valuable than the old ones? LC might be wise to publicize the answer to this question.

The same principle holds in our institutions. We shouldn't expect our patrons, or other members of the staff who receive our departmental outputs, to simply take our word for it when we say, "We're not doing Activity X anymore because it's not valuable enough to justify our time." Instead, we have to show them *how* we plan to use our time better, and we have to be able to explain *why* the new activities will be better. Before we implement the changes, we need to solicit input so that we can anticipate the potentially adverse effects and factor those effects into the cost-benefit equation. Then, having made a (hopefully) wise and well-informed choice, we have to demonstrate that the choice we made was, in fact, the best one for our patrons.

Because, after all, this isn't about rejecting old practices in favor of new ones; it's about rejecting lower-value practices in favor of higher-value ones.

NOTE

1.   Library of Congress, "The Director for Acquisitions and Bibliographic Access Announces the Library of Congress's Decision to Cease Creating Series Authority Records as Part of Library of Congress Cataloging" (April 20, 2006). The original memo has been removed from the Library of Congress website, but a copy of the text can be found at www.library. yorku.ca/cms/bibblog/2006/04/24/lc-to-stop-creating-series-authority-records.

21

Preservation, Yes—but
What Shall We Preserve?

OUR WORK AS librarians has always been the work of making difficult choices, but sometimes it seems like the choices we have to make are getting harder and harder. In this essay, I'd like to talk about one that's so tough we don't even talk about it: How do we decide what information is not worth the trouble of preserving?

As people dedicated to collecting, safeguarding, and providing access to information, and as people with a social conscience generally, we're loath to say that any one kind of information is more worthwhile than another; we see value in classical music and pop music, in canonical literature and genre fiction, in perspectives from the mainstream and from the margins.

But, as professionals, we also have to acknowledge the fact that we're being paid to discriminate. We've always had to choose between resources that are "more relevant" and "less relevant" ("Given a limited budget, should I buy a history of Massachusetts or a history of Wisconsin?") and to some degree between "better" and "worse" ("Given that my library needs a history of Wisconsin and can afford only one, which one seems most reliable, thorough, and up-to-date?"). But we've always made those decisions with the understanding that even if our library isn't going to buy that history of Massachusetts, another library will. The book isn't being lost; it's just being cared for elsewhere.

But the question "What will my individual library collect?" is subtly but significantly different from the question "What must our profession preserve?" In a way, the latter question is actually easy to answer,

---

This essay was originally published in *Against the Grain* 20, no. 5 (November 2008): 52–53.

because any answer will make us feel good: we must preserve this, and that, and the other thing, and no matter what the things are, there's almost always a good reason to preserve them. But there's another question that is just as important but much, much harder to face: What can we decide *not* to preserve? Let's not be euphemistic here: this is a question that requires us to identify information that is, as the British put it, "surplus to requirements." It requires us to identify books, journal articles, websites, opinion pieces (yikes), recipes, oral histories, photographs, blog entries, musical compositions, and other documents that we are willing to let fade into oblivion, never to be seen or heard from again. Let's be even more brutally realistic: this is not about deciding that it's okay for *my library's copy* to disappear; we're talking about deciding *what can be allowed to disappear completely from the human record*.

Now, horrifying as that sounds, it doesn't sound as bad as it could. Actively identifying information sources that can be let go at least requires the application of some measure of professional discrimination and training. It implies that we look at the whole array of what's available (or at least a significant chunk of it) and make thoughtful choices about individual documents. Unfortunately, if we're going to be realistic and hardheaded, we have to acknowledge that this is impossible.

Why? Consider this statistic: a 2003 study found that the production of "new, stored information" increased at a rate of 30 percent per year between 1999 and 2002, and that the total amount of new information created in 2002—alone—was five exabytes.[1] This means that even if all the information professionals in the world united as one in a commitment to review and categorize all (or even most of) the information produced in 2002, it could never happen. All of us probably recognize this, at some level of consciousness. But I'm not sure we all understand how monumentally impossible that task would be, or how microscopically tiny is the sliver of information output over which we have any influence as librarians.

At the risk of belaboring an obvious point, let me try to put these numbers into perspective: Five exabytes of new information were created in 2002. One exabyte of information equals one billion (that's billion, not million) gigabytes. A home computer with a 100-gigabyte hard drive can hold the equivalent of 266,650 300-page books. Assuming a world population of 6.5 billion people, five exabytes of new information translates into 20,511 new 300-page books (unique titles) per person. In 2003, OCLC estimated that there were 690,000 librarians in the world.[2] Of course, not everyone who takes care of information is a librarian, so let's double that number. No, actually, let's multiply it by

ten, giving us a processing team of 6.9 million information professionals; this assumes that worldwide one person per thousand is a member
of the information profession. If we were to charge the information
profession with reviewing, categorizing, and caring for all of the new
information created in 2002 alone, that would mean each professional
would be assigned the equivalent of just over 19.3 million books. And
that's only for 2002. Assuming that the amount of newly created and
stored information is still only increasing at a rate of 30 percent per
year, for 2003 your assignment will increase to 25 million books, and
the year after that it increases to 32.6 million. In this scenario, each
information professional would be charged with gathering and organizing the equivalent of the Library of Congress—every year.

The obvious objection to the preceding paragraph is this: "Come on,
Rick; you're poking at a straw man. No one has ever said we can capture
and take care of all the world's information." Granted. But how many
of us realize how infinitesimal is the size of what we *are* able to capture
and care for? Again: assuming—and this is an exceedingly generous
assumption—that one person in a thousand is an information professional, that person can't even come close to handling the rounding error
on his share of the world's information. Even if we allowed that only
1/100 of the Information produced worldwide each year is worthy of an
information professional's attention, that amount of information is still
completely impossible to handle.

And here's why the straw man is relevant. Elsewhere I have argued
that we, as a profession, have a tendency to argue from value while
ignoring opportunity cost—a tendency to say that we must continue
doing X because X is valuable while closing our eyes to the value of the
things that don't get done while we're doing X.[3]

What the ongoing, exponential explosion of newly created information does is massively increase, in a mostly invisible but still urgently
real way, the opportunity cost of everything that we do in the library.
Every year, the opportunity cost of doing what we did last year increases
at the rate of information growth, and that rate is already high and will
only increase further.

So what does this mean for preservation? I think it means several
things:

1. Painful as it may be to do so, we should explicitly acknowledge
   that the overwhelmingly vast majority of the world's documented
   intellectual output (what the Berkeley study called "new, stored
   information") is going to exist in the world only temporarily and

will eventually disappear permanently. This is no one's fault. It's simply the reality of a world in which creating and distributing information has recently become easy and cheap while organizing and archiving information permanently remains difficult and expensive.

2. As librarians, we must set priorities ruthlessly. Knowing that we can't keep and care for everything that deserves to be kept and cared for, we have to reallocate staff time to the care of those documents that deserve it most and dispassionately take staff time away from objects and processes that deserve it even a little bit less.

3. Bearing in mind how tiny is the fraction of information over which we can actually exercise stewardship, we should rethink the principles we use to set those priorities. How can we tell whether a document contributes substantially to our institutional mission? What makes a document more worthy of preservation than another one? Or, more to the point for each of us, what makes a document more worthy of *my staff's time* than another one? The documents that deserve it most may or may not be the ones we consider "best"; they are those that most effectively meet the needs of our patrons and help the library advance the priorities of the community it serves.

4. We must largely (though not completely) let go of our boutique model of both collecting and preserving. It's easy to leaf through a publisher's catalog and find titles that look interesting and relevant. It's easy to decide that the damaged book I see in front of me right now deserves to be repaired. It's hard even to comprehend, let alone honestly confront, the huge and growing opportunity cost imposed by directing time to those activities.

I realize that this whole essay tends to conflate the issues of preservation and collection development. But that's partly because the connection between them is so intimate. Preservation is basically the enforcement arm of collection development; it's the mechanism by which we make our collecting decisions stick. Decisions about collection development are necessarily preservation decisions, and vice versa.

I also realize that I haven't exactly proposed a real solution to the problem of preservation in an environment of overwhelmingly explosive information growth. Ultimately, there may not be a solution. We may eventually have to let go of the whole idea of the library as a permanent repository and flip the traditional collection model: instead of investing primarily in permanent collections, focus more on providing an effective portal to everything that's available at a given moment. Not even the Library of Congress can handle everything that it really ought to. Why do we continue pretending that it—let alone the rest of us—can?

NOTES

1. University of California, Berkeley, School of Information Management and Systems, "Executive Summary," in *How Much Information? 2003* (Berkeley, CA: University of California, 2003), www2.sims.berkeley.edu/research/projects/how-much-info-2003/execsum.htm.

2. OCLC, *Libraries: How They Stack Up* (Dublin, OH: OCLC, 2013), www.oclc.org/content/dam/oclc/reports/librariesstackup.pdf.

3. See essay 20 in this volume.

22

The Struggle for Library Space

IN ACADEMIC LIBRARIES, there seems to be growing concern about the problem of space—not only a lack of it in our library buildings, though that is a problem for many of us, but also the opposite: a concern that the spaces we do have are going to be (or already are being) taken over by campus entities and programs that are related only tangentially, if at all, to library services. I'm convinced that this concern is valid, and that it should actually be more widespread than it currently is. I have two reasons for thinking this.

First of all, most academic institutions spend a very large amount of money on space, capital equipment, and infrastructure in the library. Second of all, on most of these campuses, the decision to make the library a large (and in many cases enormous) building was made at a time when the library's extensive collection of printed materials constituted its most obvious value proposition on campus, and when virtually all other library services centered on the collection itself and the campus community's use of it: reference librarians helped students use the collection; technical services staff curated it and managed its growth; subject specialists kept it relevant and current; public service staff checked books in and out; collection maintenance staff reshelved them and kept them in order. At the time that most of our libraries were built, the central purpose of the library was to house, protect, and administer access to a big collection of physical documents.

Today, however, library programming and usage patterns have changed dramatically. In research libraries, a steep and ongoing decline in use of the circulating collection has been amply documented as students and faculty get access to increasing amounts of scholarly infor-

This essay was originally published as "The Battle over Library Spaces" in two columns in *Library Journal*'s *Academic Newswire*, March 27 and May 1, 2014. Reprinted by permission.

mation online (much of it brokered by the library, but an increasing amount of it available on the open Web).[1] Fewer and fewer libraries employ full-time bibliographers to shape and maintain collections, and technical services staffing is shrinking as libraries outsource routine processing tasks to vendors or to consortia. Librarians who used to sit behind desks at service points spend more and more of their time outside the library, working in classrooms and faculty offices. In many libraries, it's becoming difficult to justify the large amounts of floor space that are still dedicated to programs and processes of shrinking size or significance.

A second reason for taking seriously the concern about the loss of library space has to do with the space crunch on our campuses generally. On most academic campuses, space is at a premium; there are not enough classrooms, not enough study spaces, not enough offices. When it comes to space on campus, osmosis is a powerful force: a library in the middle of a crowded campus can no more expect its empty or underutilized spaces to stay empty than a dry sponge can expect to stay dry in the middle of a bucket of water. In such an environment, the pressure on the library to make room for other services and programs will be strong and constant, and the library administrator will be continually faced with difficult political, practical, and strategic choices. Saying "no" to a potential invader can be costly in terms of political capital; saying "yes" will likely be expensive in terms of space and opportunity cost.

So what is the right response to this challenge? Should the library try to defend its borders at all costs from any incursion? Should it simply roll over and welcome anyone who shows up at the door looking for offices or service spaces?

Having dealt with this problem repeatedly over the past few years, I've come to a few conclusions about what works well and what doesn't. Here I will propose three general principles that I've found helpful in dealing with potential incursions and then propose some concrete and practical strategies based on these principles that, in my experience, are effective for working with those who do end up taking up residence in the library.

- *Principle 1: The library does not belong to you.* When faced with a request for space in the library, it is essential that the library administrator bear in mind that the library is not an independent organization; it is a campus entity, and decisions about whether and how its space is allocated to other campus entities will ultimately be made at a level somewhere above the library. The library director who, whenever faced with a request for space in the library, says "no" on a knee-jerk basis will lose the confidence of campus administrators and will eventually be overruled by them. And at that point, the director will have no more say over what does and doesn't move into the library because the administration will have lost confidence in the director's good faith and sound judgment. This point leads directly to the next.

- *Principle 2: Say "yes" or "no" based on strategy, not on defensiveness.* Defensiveness arises from feelings of ownership and territoriality. Once those feelings are set aside, you will be ready to think in terms of strategy: Who is it that wants to take up residence in the library, and are there clear strategic or programmatic connections between what they do and what the library does? By making room for them, will the library be creating new opportunities for collaboration that improve life for everyone (and especially students)? If so—and if the space is truly available—then "yes" may well be the right answer. If not, then further discussion is in order. This point also leads directly to the next.

- *Principle 3: Cooperation creates political capital.* The more you say "yes," the more the library's reputation as a "team player" on campus will grow. And the stronger your reputation is in that regard, the more support you will have when it comes time to issue a strategic "no" to someone trying to get in. Every time you say yes, you add to your account of political capital, and every time you say no, you draw it down. If you build up your political capital by saying yes to proposals that benefit everyone anyway (even though it may sting a bit to give up space), you will then be given more latitude to say no when a proposal makes less sense—partly because you've shown yourself to be reasonable and cooperative, but also because you've demonstrated sound judgment about what will be most helpful to your academic community.

I can speak to these principles from direct experience as an interim dean. During the eighteen months that I spent leading a large research library, I was repeatedly approached by campus administrators looking for places to house faculty members or programs that needed space, usually on a temporary basis. I was also regularly approached by directors of programs that needed permanent space, who loved the library and believed (often correctly) it would be a great place for them. When the space needed was temporary and space was available, I almost always said yes; since the space was open and the need was temporary, these were invariably low-cost concessions for us, and because they often relieved acute pain and stress elsewhere on campus, these decisions generated significant political capital for the library, which in turn put us in an excellent position to be a bit more guarded when requests for permanent space came our way. Having demonstrated our willingness to help whenever we could, our concerns were then taken seriously (rather than as expressions of reflexive territoriality) when we raised them about programs that did not seem to be a good fit, or when we had to explain that what looked like empty space at the moment was actually programmed space that the library was going to need in the future.

Libraries that keep in mind the first principle mentioned above (responding to requests for space strategically rather than defensively) should find, happily, that when programs and people do end up in the library, they will usually represent initiatives that nicely complement the library's own programs and goals. For example, one partnership that my library established years ago was with our campus's Academic Advising office. We now have several cubicles housing advisors from that office in the Knowledge Commons area of our library, which brings together our major research assistance offerings with representatives of the campus's major academic support office. As tired as we all are of the overused term "synergy," that's exactly what we've achieved with this partnership.

Sometimes, however, you will find yourself in a position where it is wise to allow someone to take up space in the library despite the lack of any clear connection between the guest's program and the library's. A professor or staff employee may need temporary refuge from a difficult situation elsewhere on campus, or a program office may need somewhere to perch for a few months while a renovation project is completed. When the space request is situational and the programmatic fit is poor, these arrangements tend to be temporary.

Whether the relationship is temporary or permanent, however, living together in the same building will always entail certain challenges. Some of them are unavoidable, but all can be eased by taking certain steps and keeping certain principles in mind. These include:

- *Begin all space-sharing relationships with a formal document*, one that is signed and co-signed and that clearly lays out rights and responsibilities of both parties. (The one we use in my library can be found at http://content.lib.utah.edu/cdm/ref/collection/ir-eua/id/3118.) This agreement should be reviewed by both parties on a regular basis. The document should make it clear that some rules apply to everyone who inhabits the building, no matter where their organizational reporting lines run. These rules might include requirements to participate in safety drills, to maintain a certain level of cleanliness, to cooperate with security staff, etc.

- *Bear in mind that if the library hosts other services, patrons will likely experience them as "library services."* This means that interactions over which you have very little control are going to shape patrons' perceptions of the library. To a great degree, this is something you will simply have to accept. In some cases, it may be possible to influence the service philosophies of your partners; however, when addressing service issues with your hosted partners, be careful not to send the message "You guys are really lousy at this and we're good at it." (And, of course, bear in mind that the learning may need to flow in the opposite direction as well: the library may well be able to pick up service tips from its partners.)

- *Don't treat your guests like tenants, or even like guests; treat them like fellow citizens.* The library and its partner programs are both tenants of a building that belongs to the campus. However, since the library building is largely under the library organization's control, the library should make sure to keep its partners in the loop regarding building events, maintenance issues, changes in opening hours, custodial arrangements, etc. Announcements that go to everyone in the library organization will often not reach those who are physically located in the library but not part of the organization, so maintaining a separate e-mail list for the full population of the building itself is a very good idea.

- *Invite partners to meetings and events, maybe even on a recurring basis.* In my library, we house the Teaching and Learning Technologies (TLT) program, which includes one of the campus's major testing centers. Because this relationship is so important, and because the programmatic connections between TLT and the library are so strong, we have made it a point to invite the TLT's director to attend meetings of the library's executive leadership team on a quarterly basis. This gives our two programs a regular and predictable opportunity to update each other on initiatives and activities and to touch base about any difficulties or issues that may need to be resolved. This level of interaction and coordination won't be necessary with every relationship, but it's wise to think about it whenever a partner relationship begins.

- *There will be blood. Clean it up promptly.* Every organization has its own culture, and when two different organizations are placed in the same building, the two cultures will very likely come into conflict at some point. Acknowledge this likelihood early in the relationship, and commit together that when conflict arises, it will be dealt with promptly, professionally, and respectfully.

Further to that last bulleted point, it's important to remember that by no means will following the principles outlined above guarantee a perfectly harmonious and conflict-free relationship with your new partner in the library space. However, in our experience in my library, these principles can help a lot—both to prevent unnecessary conflict and to provide a clear path to resolution when it does arise.

NOTE

1.   Rick Anderson, "Print on the Margins," *Library Journal* 136 (June 2011): 38–39.

SECTION II

SCHOLARLY COMMUNICATION AND LIBRARY-PUBLISHER RELATIONS

23

On Advocacy, Analysis, and the Vital Importance of Knowing the Difference

HERE'S A PROPOSITION with which I suspect publishers, editors, authors, librarians, and readers would all agree: over the past couple of decades, the environment in which we all operate in these roles has become much more complex.

Here's another one that I also suspect will be uncontroversial: with the increasing complexity of the scholarly communication environment has come a greater intensity of feeling about the impacts and implications of those changes and about what we ought to do going forward. Some members of our community feel under threat, some feel exhilarated about possibilities for the future, some feel angry, some feel anxious. Many are confused and apprehensive. None of these feelings, I believe, is intrinsically uninformed or necessarily irrational, though all of us may handle our feelings in ways that are more or less useful and wise.

The increasing complexity of our environment and the heightened emotion around the issues we're dealing with suggest, I believe, the increasing importance of discriminating between analysis and advocacy. As issues become more complex, the more important it becomes to do (and listen to) careful analysis of those issues; at the same time, however, as issues become more emotionally or politically fraught, the louder will become the voices of advocacy on all sides. To be clear, the world needs both analysts and advocates; however, it's essential that we be able to discriminate between them. If we don't

This essay was originally published as "Advocacy, Analysis, and the Vital Importance of Discriminating between Them" in *The Scholarly Kitchen* (blog), July 20, 2015.

carefully do so, we run the risk of accepting propaganda as reportage or debatable interpretation as solid fact.

In the scholarly communication community, virtually every point of view has advocates, and every segment of the community produces analysis of various kinds. In the United States, publishers have advocacy groups like the Association of American Publishers (AAP), authors have the American Association of University Professors (AAUP), and libraries have the American Library Association (ALA). Analysts and analysis organizations include the Coalition for Networked Information (CNI), Outsell, Inc., and a variety of individuals who provide research, data, and consultation to all segments of the community. Some organizations have one department or subunit that acts in an advocacy role and another that does analysis; consider, for example, the Association of Research Libraries (ARL), which hosts both a Statistics and Assessment office, dedicated to the gathering and analysis of quantitative data from member libraries, and, until recently, an advocacy organization (the Scholarly Publishing and Academic Resources Coalition, or SPARC), which lobbies Congress (as well as funding agencies and the higher-education community) on behalf of policy reform.

Furthermore, the dividing line between analysis and advocacy can sometimes be tough to identify, especially when a particular analyst has a hidden agenda. Sometimes, advocacy deliberately masquerades as analysis: just because an organization calls itself a "Research Council" doesn't mean it's doing disinterested research.

Anticipating one likely objection to this essay, I want to emphasize again my view that advocacy is both good and important. However, it's essential that those of us charged with making decisions about programs, priorities, and resource allocation be able to recognize the limitations of advocacy—whatever its source or point of view—as a source of complete or reliable information.

Why would I say that? Fundamentally, because it is an analyst's job to tell the whole story, but it is an advocate's job to tell only the part of the story that will further the advocate's agenda. This becomes particularly problematic when advocates are treated in the news media as sources of analysis. (Please note that none of this means it's possible to do absolutely unbiased and objective analysis; all of us have agendas of one kind or another, not all of them conscious. However, it is in the essential nature of analysis to attempt to provide a whole and unbiased picture; it is in the essential nature of advocacy to promote a particular goal. This difference matters very much.)

How do these fundamental differences play out in the real world, and what kinds of markers can we look for when trying to discriminate between analysis and advocacy? I would suggest that they include these five:

Complexity vs. Simplicity

Analysis will tend to draw attention to complexities because a recognition of complexities (where they legitimately exist) leads to a nuanced understanding of the issue. Advocacy, on the other hand, will want to make the issue as simple as possible—partly because simple stories are easier to communicate and partly because simple stories make effective slogans. (Advocates love slogans; slogans tend to really irritate analysts.) This is not a hard-and-fast rule, of course; sometimes, voices of advocacy will try to create nuance and complexity where none exists, if the simple reality of a situation is not conducive to the advocates' agenda. But in my experience this scenario is less common than the opposite.

Data vs. Anecdote

Advocacy argues from data when the data support the agenda and argues from anecdote when supportive data are lacking or where the data's implications are too complex to unambiguously support the agenda. Analysis argues only from data, using anecdote sparingly (if at all) and only for illustrative purposes. To be clear, none of this means that anecdotes can't be tremendously useful and meaningful, particularly when used honestly and responsibly—only that (as the popular axiom has it) "the plural of anecdote is not data."

Comprehensiveness vs. Selectivity

Analysis draws on relevant information as broadly and inclusively as possible, trying to incorporate as much relevant data as it can to inform conclusions and carefully taking into account the implications of the full range of that information. Advocacy uses data selectively, emphasizing those data points that support the agenda and downplaying or leaving unmentioned those that don't support the agenda. Please note, again, that there is not necessarily anything dishonest or wrong about the latter approach; it simply reflects the fact that advocates have a very different job from that of analysts. (Of course, the selective approach can easily devolve into dishonesty if advocates are unscrupulous about the selection criteria they use when presenting data.)

Transparency vs. Opacity

Analysts will tend to share their data widely, recognizing that there may be information embedded in the data that they themselves have missed and that others may be able to tease out. Good analysts also understand that their interpretations will inevitably be shaded by their own biases and experience and that there is great interpretive value in letting others look at the same data through the lenses of their own biases and prejudices. Advocates will tend to share their data grudgingly, if at all, for exactly the same reasons.

Passion vs. Dispassion

Advocates need to be passionate because communicating the urgency and rightness of their agenda is an important part of their job. An advocate who presents his message coolly and dispassionately is arguably not doing what he should. Analysts, on the other hand, need to be dispassionate; they need to show, not only by their analysis itself but also by the manner in which it's presented, that they do not have a vested interest in any particular conclusion but are simply stating the facts as they found them. Again: we all understand that there is no such thing as a purely unbiased presentation of the facts—but the ideal toward which the analyst aspires is to present reality as dispassionately and with as much objective accuracy as possible.

24

Signal Distortion

Why the Scholarly Communication
Economy Is So Weird

FROM COLLEAGUES in the library profession, I regularly hear the assertion that the current scholarly communication system is "broken"—largely because it requires academic institutions to "buy back" their own professors' work from commercial publishers, or because it requires taxpayers to "pay twice" for research they have already funded. For reasons I've enumerated elsewhere (see essay 34 in this volume), I disagree.

I do, however, believe the system is broken—or at least fundamentally flawed—because its structure forces each participant to make choices in a vacuum or, at best, in a distortion chamber. To put it another way, each participant is a blind person with his or her hand on a different part of the elephant.

One major contributor to this problem is the fact that the journal publishing marketplace is not traditionally competitive. Journals do compete for content suppliers (authors) because every journal provides authors a functionally similar service. However, journals don't compete in the same way for buyers because every journal provides unique content; two linguistics journals may look, on the surface, like similar products offering competing value propositions to the marketplace, but in fact each offers a completely unique value proposition since the articles in each journal are unique (related to one another only in their disciplinary focus) and unavailable from any other source.

This essay was originally published in *The Scholarly Kitchen* (blog), May 14, 2013.

Choosing between two linguistics journals is, therefore, not like choosing between a Ford and a Chevrolet, both of which are products that do almost exactly the same thing and compete for your business around the margins of the driving experience (smoother drive, better gas mileage, etc.). In that competitive scenario, the buyer wants to end up with only one car and will try to choose the best one. Two linguistics journals, on the other hand, compete for your subscription money in the same way that groceries and clothing do: what you really want is to buy both, but if you don't have enough money for both, you have to make a difficult choice between them.

But the more I've thought about this issue, the more I've become convinced that the weirdness of the scholarly communication marketplace goes far deeper than the question of competition for buyers. In fact, I think the frustrations that many constituents experience with the current structure arise from the fact that each participant in the system gets fundamentally incomplete, and therefore distorted, signals from the marketplace in response to the inputs it contributes.

Here I'll focus mainly on the journal marketplace, which accounts for the great majority of dollars spent by research libraries. Books pose a somewhat different set of issues.

To invoke another metaphor and provide some comparative context, consider the marketplace for office chairs. If I can't afford a very expensive chair from Herman Miller, that doesn't mean I don't get to have a chair; it just means I have to buy a cheaper brand of chair. Herman Miller can command a very high price for its chairs only if:

a. a great many of its potential customers believe Herman Miller chairs are of very high quality, and
b. those customers have sufficient money to pay for them.

Herman Miller's ability to command those high prices will be undermined to the degree that other chair makers enter the marketplace and offer high-quality chairs as well at a lower price. If, however, Herman Miller were the only chair maker in the world, its position would be much different, and the market's responses to its pricing signals would be distorted.

This is, arguably, the position in which journal publishers find themselves. So let's start with their situation.

Journal Publishers

Journal publishers sell two services in the scholarly communication marketplace: one is a suite of offerings they sell to authors (who trade publishing rights and often their copyrights for the services of review, editing, certification, dissemination, and some degree of archiving); the other is a set of services they sell to libraries and individual subscribers (who trade money for access to articles). Author services are provided in a more or less normally competitive marketplace, because authors have a meaningful choice of venues for their work. Access, however, is not sold in a normal environment of competition, because access is controlled monopolistically. The moderating pressures that competition exerts on price increases in more conventionally competitive environments do not apply in the journals marketplace; if a publisher decides to double what it charges a customer for access, the customer does not have the option of going to a competitor for a functionally similar product. This fact severely distorts the signals a publisher receives back from the marketplace in response to any change in price and thus makes it very difficult for the publisher to know whether it is charging the "right" price.

Authors

Authors also receive partial and distorted signals from the marketplace in response to their inputs. They submit manuscripts to publishers and get feedback based purely on quality and relevance: if their submission is of high enough quality and a good enough fit for the journal, the article will be accepted, in which case the author will receive (in lieu of payment from the publisher) the benefits of editing, certification, and dissemination. The author's choice of journal has varying impacts on the marketplace depending on whether she submits to a $500 journal or a $20,000 journal—but those impacts are absorbed by other participants in the system and are not felt directly by the author. The only consequence directly experienced by the author is that of prestige and exposure (or lack thereof). An author who contributes to a journal seen by others as exploitative or "immoral" may get some negative feedback from colleagues, but this is quite unlikely—and that feedback constitutes a relatively weak signal compared to, say, seeing one's name on the contents page of the highest-ranked journal in one's field. Similarly, when an author contributes to a more "virtuous" journal, she receives no direct benefit for doing so, especially if that virtuous journal is not particularly prestigious.

Libraries

Although they don't usually characterize it this way, research libraries are selling a service in the scholarly communication system as well—or, more accurately, a suite of services. In return for institutional funding (and, often, explicitly dedicated student fees), research libraries broker access to information resources and provide a variety of support services to students and scholars. They also provide archival hosting for print backfiles and, increasingly, digital archiving of scholarly products as well. In an academic environment, journal purchasing decisions are typically made by librarians—not by the readers who will benefit directly from those decisions, though their input is often solicited. Since library budgets are limited, librarians have to cancel or forego some purchases; but since readers don't experience the impacts of price, they put pressure on the library never to cancel or to forego purchase. If the library cancels a subscription, it experiences budgetary relief—but does not feel (thought it may hear about) the pain of its constituents who have suddenly been denied access to content that may be important to their work. Librarians do typically canvass their constituents in order to gather information about the impacts of their decisions, but information gathered in this way will always be partial and only partly reliable.

Readers

On an academic campus, readers experience little or nothing of price; it is no harder for them to access a library-provided $20,000 journal than a $1,000 journal. What they do experience are relevance ("Does the library give me access to journals in my field?") and quality ("Does the library give me access to really good journals in my field?"). Since price impacts are outside the readers' experience, they will tend to push their libraries to acquire relevant and high-quality journals, no matter what they cost. Obviously, pricing levels or trends that might modify the reading behavior if readers paid the subscription bills themselves will have little, if any, impact on reading behavior when the bills are being paid by someone else. Similarly, readers (as faculty members) don't care about cancellations except those that fall within their disciplinary purview. A biologist faced with the possibility of losing access to a $5,000 journal subscription due to insufficient library funds will happily let the library cancel one or more linguistics journals in order to preserve the biology title—and vice versa.

In summary, the biggest problem I see with the existing scholarly communication marketplace is not the fact that faculty provide "free" content to journal publishers and then ask their libraries to pay for the formally published versions of those same articles. This is a natural and rational consequence of asking publishers to provide value-added services. The biggest problem is the fact that each participant in the system receives distorted and radically incomplete market responses to its inputs. There is virtually no competitive pressure on publishers to control journal prices; authors' submission decisions have significant impacts on other players that the authors themselves never feel; librarians make selection decisions but do not experience directly any of the meaningful consequences of those decisions either; readers make requests of their libraries without regard to price because they do not pay the bills.

Solutions?

It's difficult to see a solution to this problem that would not take scholarly publishing out of the commercial marketplace altogether. Some would hail such a development. I share thoughts on this idea in essay 31 of this volume.

25

Six Mistakes Your Sales Reps Are Making—and Six That Librarians Are Making

I'VE NOW BEEN dealing with sales representatives in a variety of settings for about twenty-seven years, both supporting reps as a bibliographer for a large academic book jobber and, on the other side, as a library staff member and professional librarian working in acquisitions, collection development, licensing, electronic resource management, and administrative positions. In general, I've found working with sales staff to be one of the great pleasures of my job; the vast majority of reps are skilled and smart and well-informed and helpful, and I cherish my professional association with them, some of whom have become my close friends.

Like all of us, however—librarians very much included—sales reps have a tendency to make mistakes, and over the years I've come to see patterns in those mistakes. I share six of them in this essay, followed by six common mistakes I have observed (and made myself) on the library side.

1. Telling the Company Story

I sincerely hate to tell you this, but we don't care. No one cares. It doesn't matter to us that your company was founded in 1850 and has been in the same family for generations or that it started out in a garage

---

This essay was originally published in two parts, "Six Mistakes Your Sales Reps Are Making" and "Six Mistakes the Library Staff Are Making," in *The Scholarly Kitchen* (blog), December 4, 2012, and January 10, 2013.

in Milwaukee in 1972 and has since expanded to do business in forty countries around the world. We're not going to make any purchasing decision based on your company's history, because we're not investing in your company. We're doing two things: first, we're buying a product from your company (and if we had any doubt you could provide it reliably, we wouldn't be talking to you in the first place), and, second, we're counting on a certain level of service quality (on which your company's history has relatively little bearing). If you're a vendor or aggregator competing directly with others who sell the same content as you do, then what I find much more helpful and relevant than history are statistics and references. What are your fulfillment rates? How much have your prices or service fees risen over the past ten years? Whom do you do business with now, and can we call them to find out what their experience with you has been? The answers we get to those questions are just as likely to be satisfactory coming from a 10-year-old company as from a 100-year-old one. (I can think of one exception to this rule: if your company has been passed around between five different private-equity firms over the past four years, then please do let us know that.) *Takeaway point: Don't sell us your company. Sell us your product or service, and let us get back to our jobs.*

2. Bragging to Us about Company Growth

When sales reps tell us about all the new customers coming on board, I get the impression they think we're going to be impressed and reassured to hear that the company is doing well, and that we'll feel better about our relationship with the company because we're part of an impressive and growing customer population. But when you tell us about all your new customers, what we hear is that there is now growing competition for the time and attention of your support staff. When my rep tells me that Harvard and the University of California system have joined my library in the customer population for a product or service to which I subscribe, it doesn't make me feel proud of the company I'm in; it makes me feel uncertain about whether my business is still as important to you as it was before those 500-pound gorillas joined the party, and (even more importantly) it leaves me wondering whether you are hiring additional back-office staff to handle what will surely be a significant increase in demand for their support. When you say, "Look at our growth!" I hear, "It's now going to take even longer for us to respond to you!" *Takeaway point: Never talk about customer-base growth without also talking about support-staff growth.*

3. Selling the Brand

This is particularly pointless if you're a publisher because you have no direct competitors. You may think you do, but what you really have competition for is authors, who can get comparable services from other publishers; you have no real competition for subscribers, because we can't get your content from anyone else and—more importantly—we don't make purchase or subscription decisions based on your brand strength as a publisher. No faculty member ever asks us why we don't subscribe to more Wiley journals or urges us to put more Routledge monographs in the collection. Conversely, if a faculty member says, "We must have access to *Journal X*," we almost never respond by saying, "That's not a great publisher; how about if we subscribe to a similar journal from a better publisher instead?" We generally make subscription decisions on a title-by-title basis, not a publisher basis, and in these days of extreme fiscal constraint, we almost always do it in direct response to faculty demand. It does you no good to convince us of the strength of your publishing brand. I'm not saying you shouldn't make those arguments in other venues, but in the context of a sales call with the people who actually pay the subscription bills, those arguments do you very little good. *Takeaway point: In a research library, relevance and specific local needs trump brand strength every time.*

4. Acting as if Staff Time Has No Value

This mistake is almost always inadvertent but can be both frustrating and deeply offensive to your customers. Too often, sales reps come to the library and ask for meetings with five or ten or twenty staff members, showing little sensitivity to the tremendous opportunity cost that such meetings represent. That opportunity cost grows every year because our staffs are getting smaller even as our student bodies are getting larger, our gate counts are going up, the structure of our purchasing regimes is changing, and the ways in which we bring services to campus are proliferating. If eight members of my staff attend a one-hour meeting with your sales rep, that's a full day of work that doesn't get done. This isn't to say that such meetings are never worth it; sometimes they are. It's only to say that sales reps too rarely show a sensitivity to the cost. And when the first fifteen minutes of the meeting are wasted on company history and other irrelevancies rather than useful information, the problem is compounded. *Takeaway point: Library staff time is precious. When you fail to treat it that way, you show disrespect to your customer.*

5. Responding to Affordability Statements with Value Arguments

This principle is basically the First Law of Thermodynamics of library acquisitions: the value of a product is relevant only if purchasing the product is within the realm of possibility. I once spent several years fielding pitches from a particularly aggressive sales rep who very much wanted to sell my library a backfile database at a price of roughly $150,000. When we told him that we didn't have $150,000 available for such a purchase, the response was always a long explanation of how important and valuable the database is. We couldn't have agreed more. But the value proposition doesn't make $150,000 magically appear in our budget. There was a time, in the not-too-distant past, when we had the option of canceling marginal journal subscriptions and cutting our book budgets in order to make space for high-value, high-cost purchases, but for most of us, those days are over. All we have left are core subscriptions, and our book budgets have been gutted. And on top of that, our time is under increasing pressure—so we don't have time for irrelevant conversations about the value of unaffordable products. *Takeaway point: Value and affordability have nothing to do with each other, and price trumps value every time.*

6. Making Promises the Company Can't Keep

There's an old joke about library systems vendors: A guy dies and goes to hell. He's ushered into the great hall of suffering, where he sees people writhing in torment and smells the sulfurous brimstone and feels the scorch of flames on his face. He turns to the imp at his side and says, "Wait a minute. This isn't what I was promised when we made our deal. Where's the party? Where are the beautiful women and the delicious food? Where's the music?" The imp replies, "Back then you were a prospect. Now you're a client." Now, I don't want to give the impression that sales reps are generally dishonest and misleading. In my experience, they are generally honest and straightforward. But there's a structural problem in the way vendors and publishers (and many other service providers) do business: they send reps into the field and reward them for achieving sales goals but rarely send back-office support staff—the ones who have a real, ground-level understanding of what is and isn't possible, and who will field questions and complaints from the customer after the sale has been made—with them. Sales reps have a built-in incentive to make promises first and ask questions later; support staff have a built-in incentive to make sure that any promises made are reality-based. Sending support staff on the road with sales reps is expensive, but the payoff can be tremendous—and the consequences of not doing so can be dire. *Takeaway point: Better to underpromise and overdeliver than vice versa.*

Once again, I want to reiterate my deep respect for sales reps and for the important work they do. And in the spirit of fairness, I'd now like to outline some common mistakes made by librarians and library staff in dealing with reps.

To prepare the next part of this essay, since my experience on the vendor side of this relationship is much more limited than my experience on the library side, I polled a bunch of my friends and colleagues who work for publishers, subscription agents, database vendors, and other sellers of content and services to libraries. I received a tremendous(!) amount of very helpful input, the sources of which—for obvious reasons—I promised I would keep confidential. So I want to start by thanking the anonymous many who contributed significantly to the content of this essay. Since many of my informants contributed similar ideas, I've boiled down the responses and put them in my own words (so there's no use in doing a wordprint analysis to see if your sales rep was among the respondents and is talking about you). I've also limited myself to those responses that had most specifically to do with librarian-rep interactions; I received many interesting and potentially useful comments on library philosophy and practice more generally but, for the most part, decided that those are outside the scope of this particular piece.

What follows, then, is a combination of things boiled down into six bulleted points: the most commonly reported and (in my estimation) the most important mistakes that library staff are making in their dealings with sales reps. And for the record, I will admit right up front that I've been guilty of each of them at some point—some of them, I'm very embarrassed to say, more than once.

1. Rudeness/Unprofessionalism

Let's begin with the most egregious and patently unacceptable of the mistakes listed here: rude and unprofessional behavior. Examples include treating a sales rep or customer service staffer with discourtesy or derision, treating the rep like one's personal therapist, unilaterally inviting a spouse or friend to a meal hosted by the rep, and failing to show up for appointments on time (or at all). None of us, of course, is perfect—but I have to confess that as a member of the library profession, I found myself ashamed by some of the behavior that was described to me in confidence by my vendor-side informants. Apart from the fact that unprofessional behavior is never acceptable, I think sometimes we on the library side forget that when it comes to courtesy and professionalism, we have an advantage: as customers, we can very often get away with behavior that would get a sales rep fired. We should keep that advantage in mind and let our awareness of it temper our responses when frustrated or irritated. This is not to say, of course, that we should fail to be direct and clear when communicating frustration or irritation or working to solve problems—only that we should be very careful not to confuse clarity and directness with rudeness and abuse. *Takeaway point: Do unto others as you would have them do unto you.*

2. Squandering One's Time with the Rep

Wasting the rep's time by forgetting a meeting or spending it on personal complaints falls under the category of rudeness and unprofessionalism, but squandering the time one has with the rep is a different matter. This is about failing to take into account the extremely limited opportunities that one has to work in person with the sales rep and, consequently, spending that time on activities that could and should have taken place before the meeting, or on conversations that could just as easily take place by e-mail, or on issues that would be better addressed with a member of the customer service staff. Another common manifestation of this problem is taking up meeting time with conversations or arguments that are of purely internal significance. Meetings with the sales rep are not the time to argue about internal workflows, budget allocations, collection development strategies, personality conflicts, and management style. It's unprofessional to have family quarrels in front of a guest—but, more importantly, to do so is to waste a scarce resource: face time with your rep. (See also Failure to Prepare for Meetings, below.) *Takeaway point: Treat your time with the sales rep as the scarce and valuable commodity it is, and be prepared to make it maximally useful.*

3. Knee-Jerk Adversarialism and Distrust

Many of my vendor-side informants bemoaned what they feel is a knee-jerk adversarialism on the part of many librarians and their staff. Now, some library-side readers will roll their eyes ("Of course our relationship is adversarial; you want our money and we want what's best for our patrons"), but the reps have a point. As rhetorically convenient as it might be to cast the library-vendor relationship as one of white hats vs. black hats, it should be obvious to any reflective person that the reality is far more complex than that. There is a broad spectrum of public-mindedness among publishers and vendors (just as there is a broad spectrum of patron-centeredness among librarians), and most reps come to the library with a genuine desire to provide good and useful service to your patrons. Do they want to get paid? Of course they do, and so do we. When working with sales reps, it's wise to start from an assumption of honesty and good faith, and move forward from there. If you find that assumption being proved wrong, then ask for a new rep—but in the meantime, treat the relationship like the partnership it should be. *Takeaway point: Give your rep the benefit of the doubt. If he or she betrays that trust, ask for a new rep.*

4. Failure to Prepare for Meetings

Before you meet with your sales rep, prepare an agenda. Send it to the rep ahead of time, and invite him or her to contribute to it. Know what will be discussed, prepare any documentation that will be needed in order for the meeting to be productive, and know what you hope to accomplish by the end of the meeting (as well as how you'll know whether it was accomplished). If the rep provides spreadsheets, analyses, or specs ahead of time, you and your staff should read them beforehand so you're not wasting time in the meeting trying to absorb the information they contain. Well before the meeting, figure out which staff members need to be present in order for the meeting to be productive and useful—as well as which staff members do *not* need to be there. As librarians, it can be tempting to see a sales visit as a mere interruption or (more positively) as a break from work. In reality, it's an opportunity—and a relatively rare one—to get certain kinds of work done. *Takeaway point: A meeting without an agenda is just a conversation. Do your homework, and organize your time.*

5. Failure to Prepare the Ground for Product Consideration

One of the surest ways to waste both your time and that of your sales rep is to instigate trial access for a product that you know perfectly well you will never purchase, or for which it is not clear that there is real demand. Trials and pilot programs create work on both sides of the sales equation, and it's important that the investment not be wasted. To be clear: this absolutely does not mean that every trial or pilot should result in a purchase. A successful trial is one that results in a good purchasing decision, and the decision may be either positive or negative. But a trial is unlikely to be successful in that sense if the ground for it has been poorly prepared, if those whose input is required have not been given adequate notice, if the availability of trial access isn't effectively publicized, or if the analysis of the trial's outcomes is casual or ill-conceived or colored by personal prejudice. And it should (but sadly can't) go without saying that once the trial is completed, the rep needs to be informed promptly of the library's decision. *Takeaway point: Don't waste time on a trial or pilot unless you're giving the product a genuine chance.*

6. Putting Political Library Concerns above Patron Needs

I've saved for last the "mistake" that I know is likely to be the most controversial, but I think it must be said. It has long seemed to me (and comments from my vendor-side informants seem to confirm it) that too often, we in libraries put politics ahead of mission and service. By "politics," I mean our personal views about how the world ought to be, and more specifically our views about how the scholarly communication economy ought to be structured. Again, I realize that this is a very complicated, even fraught, issue, and I also realize that one's beliefs about how scholarly communication ought to be shared will inevitably have some effect on the purchasing decisions one makes on behalf of the library and its constituents. The question isn't whether politics ought to enter into such decisions. The question is one of balance. More specifically, the question is, "To what degree is it appropriate to sacrifice the short-term good of our patrons in the pursuit of long-term economic reform in scholarly publishing (or vice versa)?" In too many cases, it seems to me that we are making that sacrifice in an ill-advised way. *Takeaway point: The politics of scholarly communication is important, but the time and place for rhetoric is probably not a sales rep's visit.*

26

Prices, Models, and Fairness

A (Partly) Imaginary Phone Conversation

[*The phone on a librarian's desk rings. He picks it up.*]

Librarian: Hello?

Sales Rep: Hello! Robert from Acme Scholarly Journals here. As you know, for the past year we've been working on a new pricing model for our journal package, and now that it's ready my boss and I would like to come visit your library and explain it to you.

Librarian: Things are pretty busy here. Can you just explain it to me quickly over the phone or send me the information by e-mail?

Rep: We'd really like to deliver the explanation in person, since the new model is kind of complicated and we want to make sure you and your staff understand it.

Librarian: The thing is, a meeting like that will be very expensive for me. If I'm there with three of my staff and the meeting takes an hour, that ties up four staff hours—that's half a day's work that won't get done while we learn about your pricing model. At the end of the meeting we might understand the model, but how does that really help me?

Rep: It will help you because you'll understand why the pricing model is changing and how it works. You'll understand that your new price isn't just a number that we picked out of the air.

Librarian: I'll take your word on that. I'm sure you guys invested a lot of time and thought in coming up with your new pricing model. The thing is, the logic and structure of your pricing model don't ultimately make much difference to me. What matters is the price my library

This essay was originally published in *Against the Grain* 23, no. 1 (February 2011): 8–10, and subsequently in *The Scholarly Kitchen* (blog), March 3, 2011.

ends up with. If the price is acceptable, then how you guys arrived at the price doesn't matter that much. And if it's not acceptable, then the model still doesn't matter. Ultimately, all that matters is the price.

Rep: But one of the purposes of our new model is to make pricing more equitable. Doesn't it matter to you whether we're setting prices fairly across institutions?

Librarian: All other things being equal? Yes, I like fairness a lot. But I strongly suspect that "more equitable pricing across institutions" really just means higher pricing for my institution, and that kind of complicates my feelings about fairness and equity in this case.

Rep: The problem is that some very similar institutions are paying radically dissimilar prices, and we want to normalize the pricing structure.

Librarian: And I have no problem with that, especially if you plan to normalize it by lowering the prices for some of your customers. But I'm guessing that isn't your plan, because if it were, you wouldn't be flying reps all over the country to explain it. No one would ask you to justify a price decrease.

Rep: Actually, the price *will* decrease for some customers—but you're right, in your case the model results in a higher price. It's a price that we feel more accurately reflects the true value of our product.

Librarian: But, in reality, all that means is, "We think we can get more money for our product than we're currently getting." No vendor or publisher thinks its product is overpriced, any more than I'm likely to think I'm overpaid. When you say you're making the price more "fair" or more reflective of your product's value, what you mean is that you're raising it.

Rep: In your case, that's true. But we're not just arbitrarily raising the price of our existing product; the higher price also reflects significant investments we've made in improvements to our platform and infrastructure over the past few years. Surely you don't object to us recouping the significant expense of product improvement.

Librarian: I don't object in principle, but the problem is that there's a real logical gap between investment and value. You can say what you've invested, but only your customers can say whether the investment resulted in additional value. What if you've improved your product in ways I don't care about? What if the things you believe are improvements actually annoy my patrons and staff? Is it fair that I have to pay for changes that are worth nothing to me? What I'd like to do is continue using the old version, at the old price—I don't suppose that's an option, is it?

Rep: No. The fact is, we're not a high-margin company; we really do try to keep our costs low and our prices reasonable, and we can't support two platforms at once. It would just be too expensive, and ultimately it would drive prices up further for everyone, including those who are perfectly happy with the new platform.

Librarian: Okay, I can understand that. It doesn't make me feel any better about paying more for a product that is no more valuable to me than it was last year, though.

Rep: But I think there's something you're forgetting: your subscriptions are cumulative. If our product is valuable to you at all, then it does grow in value every year—because the content grows every year. Since we host the content for you, that means our local costs grow every year as well. Do you expect us never to raise our prices?

Librarian: No—you're right that it wouldn't be reasonable to expect prices to stay completely level. But our materials budget was cut last year and is flat this year. We can argue all we want about whether and by how much prices "should" go up; the bottom line is that I have less money this year than last, and with annual publisher price increases I'll have even less next year. I also have fewer staff, which is why I can't invest half a day's work time in listening to you and your boss explain a pricing model that doesn't ultimately matter to me. Would you please just send me the new pricing information so my staff and I can figure out how we're going to deal with it?

Rep: Okay, fine. I'm e-mailing you a document that summarizes the new model and shows your bottom-line price. You should get it in just a second.

Librarian: Yup, got it. [*Quickly calculating . . .*] Let's see: it looks like your model will result in a 40 percent price increase for my library.

Rep: We realize that the new model will require some adjustment for you, so we've prepared a five-year "glide path." Your price will go up by a smaller percentage every year until you've arrived at the new model.

Librarian: "Glide path"? That's not a glide path; it's a mountain climb. The mountain may be terraced, but still . . .

Rep: I realize this is a challenge, but that's the price that the model dictates.

Librarian: You're referring to "the model" as if it were a tyrannical third party over which you have no control. What you call "the model" is really just the price, and the price is set entirely by your company. No one is forcing you to increase my library's price by 40 percent.

Rep: Well, like I said, this is a price that levels the playing field among our customers and better reflects the value of our product. At the price we're proposing, based on your historical usage patterns, each download will cost you about $2.50. That seems like a fair price and good value for money, doesn't it?

Librarian: Actually, it does. Your journals are heavily used and in high demand here, and $2.50 per article is a good price.

Rep: So what's the problem? If you're getting a good product at a good price, why are we arguing?

Librarian: Because I can't afford it. It may be a great deal and a valuable product, but those facts don't make money magically appear in my budget. Value and affordability have no relationship to each other. You could offer me a nice four-bedroom house for $50,000, and that might be an amazing deal, but if I don't have $50,000, it doesn't matter.

Rep: But I bet you've got other subscriptions that offer much lower value than ours do, even at the higher price. Maybe you should cancel some of those to make room in your budget for our journals, which you just said are of high quality and in high demand.

Librarian: That might have been true five years ago, but it's not true anymore. Due to budget cuts and price hikes like this one, our subscription list is actually shrinking every year, and there's no longer anything we can cut without significantly hurting our users' ability to do their research. We have a couple of large package deals that involve a lot of waste, but we can't cancel those because the individual titles we need from those publishers would cost us more than the package does.

Rep: Sounds like we're at a stalemate.

Librarian: No, unfortunately, there's no such thing. If you insist on a 40 percent price increase, then we'll have to cancel some of your journals. There's just no other option. Some of our faculty will be furious, but at this point, there's no choice available to us that won't make faculty furious.

Rep: We'd really like to come visit you and talk about this some more, maybe help you see why this price increase makes sense.

Librarian: How about this: you guys come and talk to the faculty members whose departments will be directly affected by the journal cancellations that are going to be made necessary by your price hike?

Rep: [*Dial tone* . . .]

Librarian: Hello?

27

Print-on-Demand and the Law
of Unintended Consequences

SOMETIMES I TELL people that I'm haunted by the iPod. When it first came out, most of us looked at it and basically said, "Oh, how fun; it's a digital Walkman." We figured it would do just what a Walkman did—give people an easy and private way to listen to their albums while they walked around—the difference being that it could hold multiple albums at once and the music would be loaded and saved digitally. And that was a perfectly reasonable assessment of the situation; there was no particular reason to expect that the iPod was, with the introduction of iTunes, going to take us from an album-based music economy back into a song-based one and thereby massively disrupt the record industry (before giving birth to the iPhone and thereby revolutionizing both mobile computing and the marketplace for telephone services).

The iPod wasn't the only disruptive influence on the music industry, of course (massive piracy played a significant role as well), but the enduring impact of iTunes has been to re-create the music industry in the image of 1960. And what's scary about this, to me anyway, is not just that it was *unpredicted*, but that it was most likely *unpredictable*.

This is scary to me for two reasons: first, because I am currently in charge of a large research library; second, because I'm still about twenty years away from retirement age. These facts fill me with a certain sense of urgency, because research libraries are not nimble. We were never intended to be nimble; we were intended to be monumental, solid, and immovable. This made very good sense for many centuries, during which the information we were charged with gathering and organizing

---

This essay was originally published in *Academic Newswire*, February 21, 2013. Reprinted by permission.

was encoded in monumental, solid, and hard-to-move physical objects (which were simultaneously fragile and vulnerable to the elements and the predations of thieves). A lack of nimbleness implies the need for preparation, so that when threats or disruption appear, we'll be positioned to deal with them. But preparation also requires prediction, and prediction is a sucker's game.

In the January 2013 issue of the *New Criterion*, managing editor James Panero writes engagingly and insightfully about what he calls "the culture of the copy," describing the dynamics of technological (as distinct from cultural and political) revolutions and teasing out some of the many deep implications for written culture of the technological changes brought on by the Internet.[1]

For the most part, Panero casts the Internet version of "copying" (which is built on digital transmission) opposite the print-based copying that characterized the 1,600 years of the post-Gutenberg print era. I find it interesting, however, that he gives such short shrift to print-on-demand (POD)—a form of copying that stands with one foot firmly in our analog past and the other in our digital, networked present and future. The ability to make a desired book appear, physically, on demand and essentially out of thin air within minutes of expressing that desire is breathtakingly new and has the potential to be deeply, deeply disruptive to virtually everything about the businesses of bookselling and librarianship. Scalable and widely distributed POD capabilities would fully obviate the very concept of the print run and would cast into serious question the function of most library collections. And those are only the clearly predictable consequences of such a development— unsettling as they are, it's the wholly unpredictable ones that really keep me up at night, precisely because I don't even know what to worry about.

How much should libraries and publishers worry about such disruption? A lot. The mechanism for these changes already exists, in the form of centralized, warehouse-based POD and—even more exciting and disturbing—local POD devices like the Espresso Book Machine (EBM), which can print and bind a 500-page book in roughly five minutes at a cost of about one cent per page.

If these exist already, why have they failed to disrupt the industry? In the former case—warehouse-based POD fulfillment—they actually have, though quietly (so far). Some publishers, such as Oxford University Press, fulfill many backlist orders by POD. This means there is no need for a book ever to go out of print, nor for a publisher ever to commit to another print run of a backlist title. As anyone who has worked in the book industry can tell you, these are seismic changes.

As for local POD—which has not yet significantly disrupted either publishing or librarianship—what makes the EBM and similar machines potentially so disturbing is the fact that they connect to a networked database of e-books. The EBM is like a spigot attached to the side of a vat containing multiple millions of books; twist the faucet and out comes your book. Until the creation of the EBM, no individual has ever actually had ready access to anywhere near that many books. So why has the disruption not yet happened? Because, for now, the machines are very expensive and the metadata required to make the millions of digitized books actually findable is crude to nonexistent.

However, neither of these problems is likely to last. Together, they constitute a thin wall holding back a flood of easy and instant access to information that was, for hundreds of years, virtually unfindable and practically inaccessible to the vast majority of the world's population. When—not if—it suddenly becomes available to everyone with an Internet connection and can be printed affordably and on demand on a widely distributed network of POD machines, we can expect the consequences to be both enormous and largely unpredictable.

NOTE

1.   James Panero, "The Culture of the Copy," *New Criterion* 31 (January 2013): 4–9.

28

Quality and Relevance

A Matrix Model for Thinking about
Scholarly Books and Libraries

Scholarly Quality: All Ye Know and All Ye Need to Know?

In the ongoing conversation about the current and future health of the marketplace for scholarly monographs, there tends to be a lot of discussion around the issue of quality. This is understandable. Quality is a very comfortable topic for all concerned since (with relatively few exceptions) scholarly books don't generally get all the way through the editorial gauntlet of serious publishers unless they're works of pretty high quality. Publishers, authors, readers, and librarians would all agree on that, I think.

For some commentators, this seems to be pretty much all one needs to know: if the books are of high scholarly quality, then this means that (a) they should be published and (b) they should be bought—if not by individual readers (the taste and discernment of individuals being notoriously inconsistent), then at least by libraries, whose job, these commentators believe, is to discriminate between high-quality and low-quality books, and to buy the high-quality ones—thus providing essential support to good authors and publishers, building rich and coherent collections, and ensuring that the libraries' patrons (both current and future) will have access to quality resources as they pursue their scholarly work.

This essay was originally published in *The Scholarly Kitchen* (blog), September 29, 2014.

Quality vs. Resources

There's a problem, though. (Isn't there always?) It's the problem of limited resources. There may be some academic libraries out there that can afford to buy, shelve, and permanently curate every high-quality scholarly book published, but if there are, then they must be vanishingly few. Most—virtually all—academic libraries have to make tough choices about which high-quality scholarly books they'll buy and which ones they won't. This means that they have to make choices based on some variable other than quality. That variable is—and has always been, though we haven't always said so very explicitly—relevance.

What does "relevance" mean in this context? It's simple: relevance is the measure of a particular book's ability to meet real-time, real-life scholarly needs *at the purchasing institution*. The quality of a particular book doesn't vary at all from library to library; a great book is a great book, no matter who owns it. The relevance of a particular book, however, varies greatly from place to place. And this is where the conversation gets less comfortable, because while we can pretty much all agree that scholarly monographs tend to be of high quality, it is also very often true that they are quite narrow in focus. And this, in turn, means that if libraries apply relevance as a criterion in their book selecting, they will actively decide against purchasing some scholarly books, despite those books' high quality. This seemed less problematic to publishers when librarians (whose selections were driven by considerations of both quality and *potential and future* relevance) were selecting books; now that books are being increasingly purchased as a result of patron behavior (which tends to be driven by *actual and present* relevance), there is a very real risk that fewer high-quality books are going to sell.

A Matrix Model

Lately I've found myself starting to think in terms of simple two-dimensional matrices that illustrate the confluence and interaction of multiple variables. Figure 1 is an example of one such matrix that illustrates the interaction of quality and relevance in the context of scholarly book purchasing.

In the past, when libraries were relatively richly funded (and when there were fewer journals and journal prices were lower), libraries were able to buy a much higher percentage of the books that fell solidly into the high-Q/high-R quadrant of this matrix—and we also had the luxury of buying quite a few books the relevance of which was less clear but which were nevertheless of high quality. During this period, our

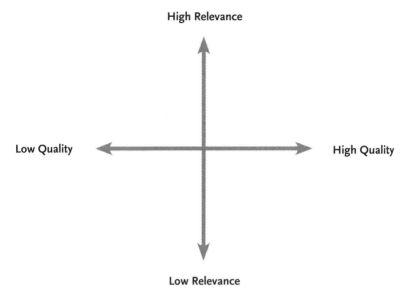

High Relevance

Low Quality   High Quality

Low Relevance

Figure 1

purchases were more broadly distributed across two quadrants: up
and down the "Relevance" vector and around the "High" end of the
"Quality" vector. Today, I think, our purchases would be more tightly
clustered around the "High" end of the "Relevance" vector, though still
fairly concentrated at the "High" end of the "Quality" vector.

Relevance Trumps Quality

It's worth noting, however, that all research libraries contain at least
some low-quality books—and this is not only because librarians failed
to notice that they were of poor quality. It's also because a book can hold
value to students and researchers that goes beyond its intrinsic scholarly qualities. Poorly written books filled with bad argumentation and
even evil intent (e.g., *Mein Kampf*) may nevertheless provide an indispensable window on the thinking of important and influential figures
in history; books containing lies masquerading as biography (*A Million
Little Pieces*) may be important sources of information on sociological
or cultural trends; deliberately fraudulent scholarship (*Arming America*)
may still valuably illustrate strains of thinking and rhetoric in public
discourse on important issues. Similarly, the greatest book in the world
in a discipline not served by a particular academic library is likely to
be a poor purchase, whereas a more mediocre book that supports the

institutional mission very directly may be a wise purchase. The bottom line here is that it's a myth that the library exists to curate and showcase the best in scholarship; in reality, the library exists to facilitate new scholarship—and new scholarship requires access to more than just what is good and true.

What this all means is that no good research library will limit itself strictly to high-quality books. Relevance is not only a *restrictive* factor on which high-quality books we choose to buy with our limited funds; it's also an *inclusive* factor when it comes to considering mediocre or low-quality books.

As I said above, when we turn from the issue of quality (which makes everyone feel good) to the issue of relevance (which makes us more nervous), the conversation becomes less comfortable. Scholarly publishers don't like the idea of libraries buying mediocre books because that's not what they sell; and they don't like the idea of libraries declining to purchase niche books because that is very often what they do sell.

The Law of Potential Relevance

All of this begs an important question, though: How can you really judge the relevance of a book? A book that seems niche-y or only peripherally important today may turn out to be highly relevant (and even prescient) tomorrow—and if not tomorrow, then maybe ten years from now, or twenty.

This is a true statement, but it's not a good point. Why? Here I will introduce the Law of Potential Relevance: *There is no document about which one cannot say, "Someday this document may be essential."* Here's the corollary to that law: *Since potential future relevance is functionally unlimited, potential future relevance is an inappropriate criterion to apply when allocating limited resources.*

Here's another way of thinking about it: The further one looks into the future, the more possible scenarios there are. And the more possible scenarios there are, the more potential there is for any given book to be relevant to one of them. This means that if you try to build a collection based on *potential future relevance*, you had better have an unlimited book budget and an infinitely expandable library—because that's the only way you'll be able to do it.

The Importance of Being Patron-Driven

What's the alternative? The alternative—which is really the only fiscally responsible and sustainable approach—is to build the collection that makes the most sense in terms of real, current, demonstrable needs, recognizing that your collection-building strategy will need to be adjusted over time. And right now, one of the most effective and least wasteful ways to do that is by putting real, current, academically active library patrons in the driver's seat when it comes to selecting books. Given that this represents a radical departure from centuries-old library practice (and from the assumptions that have guided publishing decisions for centuries as well), we can expect that such a move will continue to be controversial and difficult—for librarians and publishers, anyway. Maybe less so for researchers and students.

29

No Such Thing as A Bad Book?

Rethinking "Quality" in the Research Library

I'M GOING TO suggest something that may seem kind of crazy on its face: research libraries need to worry less about the objective quality of the books they acquire and instead focus on another property, at once more concrete and more elusive—utility. The obvious and reasonable retort to such a suggestion would be, "How useful can a low-quality book be?" Read on.

Let's start by considering two books, both of which, one could reasonably argue, are objectively bad, though each in a different way. One is a book of popular punditry, the other a scholarly monograph.

The first is *Slander: Liberal Lies about the American Right*, by political commentator Ann Coulter. This book asserts that liberals "have been wrong about everything in the last century" and that conservatives "are the most tolerant (and long-suffering) people in the world." According to Coulter, every—that's *every*—"pernicious idea to come down the pike is instantly embraced by liberals." On the other hand, all—that's *all*—new ideas that have emerged in the past twenty years have "bubbled up from the right wing." (Thank you, right wing, for the iPod, the tablet computer, and the open-access movement.) Coulter also informs us that liberals, by definition, regard ethical principle as "nothing; winning is everything." Her book teems with these kinds of breathtaking howlers, along with breezy factual misstatements, moral analogies that can charitably be characterized as bizarre, and gratuitous personal attacks on individuals with whose politics she disagrees. Even those who share

---

This essay was originally published in two parts, "Rethinking 'Quality' in the Research Library" and "Part 2: Implications and Problems," in *The Scholarly Kitchen* (blog), November 28 and December 12, 2011.

her political views have pointed out the fundamental flaws in this book.[1] One does not have to disagree with her politics to find *Slander* bad by any number of objective standards.

The second example is *Arming America: The Origins of a National Gun Culture,* by Michael Bellesiles. This book presents an argument as to the nature and extent of gun ownership in seventeenth- and eighteenth-century America. Bellesiles's thesis is that a broad gun culture did not develop in the United States until after the Civil War; before then, gun ownership was relatively rare. The book was received warmly, particularly by advocates for stricter gun control, and Bellesiles was awarded the Bancroft Prize in 2001. However, significant elements of his research fell apart under critical examination.[2] Nor were the book's problems simply a matter of poorly formulated arguments or irresponsibly selective data: some of the documents Bellesiles cited did not exist, he misquoted critical documents that did exist, and his math was in several important instances inexcusably wrong. In the wake of these revelations the prize was revoked, Bellesiles was formally investigated by Emory University, where he was a full professor (he resigned), and he was called a "fraud," "a liar," and "a disgrace" by prominent reviewers who had previously championed his work.[3]

So here's the question: Should a research library acquire these books? And in the case of the Bellesiles book, having acquired it before its dishonesty was uncovered, should a research library keep it or withdraw it?

The answer is going to depend on what one believes is the fundamental purpose of a research library. If the library's fundamental purpose is to offer its users a well-crafted repository of the world's best thinking and research on topics of interest to its users, then you could make a very strong case that neither of these books should be included. Ann Coulter's book, though it may offer some accurate critiques and maybe even a perceptive insight or two, is so padded with know-nothing bloviation and irresponsible name-calling that it completely undermines its own authority as a citable source. Bellesiles's book also probably contains some good and useful information; unfortunately, there's so much deliberate fabrication and misrepresentation in the book that it can't be trusted as an independent source either. If the library exists to give people access to high-quality documents, then neither of these books belongs in a library.

However, I'm here to argue that the library's purpose is not to give people access to high-quality documents but, rather, to give people access to useful documents—or, more to the point, to connect its users with the documents they need in order to do their work. And there are all kinds of very good work that can be supported by *Slander* and *Arming America*, as well as by other equally terrible books and articles that are bad for a whole variety of reasons. *Slander* may be a really lousy source of information about the moral and intellectual standing of the American left, but it's an excellent example of a particular type of political discourse that has emerged in the late twentieth and early twenty-first centuries. The roots of this discourse can be traced very far back in our nation's history (and before), and there is a fascinating thread that can be traced from, for example, seventeenth- and eighteenth-century colonial American broadsides and cartoons up through the nativist movements of the nineteenth century, the early radio demagoguery of the twentieth century, and the print and radio fulminations of figures like Coulter, Glenn Beck, and Rush Limbaugh more recently. I don't see how a library could support research into modern political discourse without offering patrons access to books like *Slander*.

Similarly, *Arming America* is a terrible source for accurate information about gun ownership in early America. But it seems to me that it's an indispensable resource for a researcher seeking to understand the rhetoric of gun control in the America of the twentieth century. Terrible as it is, it's a book that had a huge impact and significantly affected the conversation about gun ownership in this country, and to understand what has happened with that conversation in the years since, one would need access to that book (among many others, of course). *Arming America* is also potentially useful as a cautionary example for undergraduate journalism and history students: I can imagine a professor profitably assigning students to examine the arguments made in the book, chase down some of the miscited sources, and explain what they find. How did this author twist and misrepresent his findings? How would you have characterized the sources if you were writing this book? What are your legitimate options when faced with sources that directly contradict your thesis or your assumptions?

In other words, *Slander* and *Arming America* are not just useful *despite* their badness; they're useful precisely *because of* their badness, because their badness is of a particularly instructive type. None of this is to say that quality doesn't matter or that it's irrelevant to researchers; it's to say that quality is only one of many factors that can make a book useful to people doing scholarly work, and that other factors may well outweigh it.

Of course, it's all well and good to say that libraries should acquire books based on usefulness rather than focusing on quality. But, in practice, there are several real problems with such an approach.

First of all, librarians are in a bad position to judge usefulness. A book may be useful to a patron for any number of reasons that can't be anticipated by someone else, even if that someone else has a library degree and decades of experience doing collection development. Any book could turn out to be useful, depending on the task at hand. The traditional library collection is populated almost entirely by predictions made by librarians; the books in the collection represent librarians' collective attempts to guess what their patrons will need in the future. But since actual usefulness is highly unpredictable, we've been forced historically to treat quality as a proxy for usefulness. "We'll buy this good book rather than that bad book," we've implicitly said, "because a good book is going to serve our patrons' needs better than a bad one"—this despite the obvious fact that a high-quality book on a topic irrelevant to the patron's needs may well be of far less utility than a relevant and mediocre one, or even a very bad one that is bad in useful and instructive ways.

Second, although quality is a relatively stable property, usefulness is not. A very good biography of Theodore Roosevelt may be superseded in usefulness by a later one, but it won't become a worse book than it was just because the new one is better. At the same time, the usefulness of a particular book will not only vary greatly from user to user but is also likely to vary over time for an individual user. A software manual, for example, will be very useful to some patrons and completely useless to others—and when a new version of the software is released, the old manual may become effectively useless to the ones for whom it was very useful before. Similarly, the Roosevelt biography may be an essential resource for a graduate student today but become much less useful to her next year after her thesis is accepted. And if it's superseded by a later biography, it will become less useful to some patrons than it was beforehand, despite its continued high quality.

Third is the problem of rationing access. Historically, research librarians have rationed access by deciding how much of what kind of material should be in the collection, and we discriminated according to reasonably consistent criteria: relevance to the curriculum, price, quality, etc. As a result, our libraries now boast excellent and well-crafted collections—large chunks of which are never used, partly because despite their quality as collections, they don't contain the very specific materials particular students and researchers need in order to do their work.[4] This is the inevitable result of trying to guess what other people will want. But suppose, for the sake of argument, that librarians actually were able to figure out a way to discriminate based on utility rather than quality. How then would we allocate our acquisition budgets? Do the needs of a junior faculty member take precedence over the needs of an undergraduate student? How about the needs of a tenured faculty member versus those of an untenured one? Or of a Nobel laureate as compared with those of a postdoctoral fellow? Libraries have never provided everything that everyone needed; to do so would be impossible, even with a generous budget.

Possible solutions to the first two problems have begun emerging in recent years. First, given the impossibility of predicting the usefulness of particular books to library patrons, valuing usefulness over quality will tend to lead us to let patrons select the books we purchase rather than to continue selecting them on behalf of patrons. This obviously implies a program of patron-driven access. While I don't advocate the wholesale abandonment of speculative and librarian-driven acquisition for all libraries, I do think that this reality—the impossibility of guessing what will and won't be useful—suggests the importance for most research libraries of exploring patron-driven access models, and even doing so quite aggressively. Given the option of knowing for certain that a book will be used, why choose instead to buy one that runs a strong likelihood of not being used? Patron-driven models are enormously disruptive to the traditional library, of course. But, as librarians, our responsibility is to serve our patrons well, not to preserve the structures with which we've become comfortable.

Second, as for the unevenness (across patrons) and instability (over time) of usefulness: The implications of this reality are fairly clear, but alarming. They suggest an argument against building permanent collections at all. If usefulness is of central importance, then permanence of access should take a back seat to fluidity; the point becomes not so much to build a defined and carefully crafted collection as to create a space in which patrons can gain access to a much larger and more loosely crafted "collection," the contents of which might be to a great degree shifting and dynamic over time. Permanent access would be established (if at all) for only those materials that get used. Such an approach would mark another truly radical and fundamental change in the traditional understanding of what constitutes a research library; it would signal a shift from the model of the library as collection to one of the library as conduit—again, an extremely disruptive and even threatening structural shift for librarians.

Rationing presents perhaps the stickiest problem of the three. In the past, libraries rationed in a highly impersonal manner: we subscribed to Journal X but not Journal Y and bought Monograph A but not Monograph B, and for the most part no one took such choices personally. Everyone (well, most everyone) understood that the library's resources were limited and that hard choices had to be made for the good of the collection and its users. But switching the focus from quality to usefulness implies opening up many more options to patrons without any promise of new money. How can scarce resources be allocated carefully and wisely within such a structure? Will patrons themselves be evaluated and found more or less deserving of support depending on their status and the relevance of their work to institutional priorities? If not, then what will be the means of discrimination, given that discrimination remains essential wherever needs outstrip resources (which is to say everywhere)? A new system of resource rationing might be less disruptive to librarians, but much more disruptive to library patrons.

I confess that I have no real answer to that last question. For one thing, the complexity of a more rational allocation mechanism—one that accounts not only for the differing needs of different classes of users but also for the priorities of the institution served by the library— would be mind-boggling. For another, I can think of no strategic and need-based allocation mechanism that wouldn't ignite a firestorm of controversy among library patrons, many of whom would be outraged at the apparent unfairness of an allocation structure that explicitly privileges some disciplines and some individuals over others. Such a structure would bring to the surface a reality that has always existed, but which we generally prefer not to discuss in the context of library service: in every institution of higher education, some disciplines matter more than others, and different classes of students and employees can expect different levels of collections support. I honestly have no idea how to resolve this particular problem.

To sum up: It's human nature to emphasize the importance of what you can do well (such as judging quality) and minimize the importance of what you do poorly (judging usefulness). In the days when building speculative collections was the only way to meet patrons' needs, librarians could get away with that approach to a greater degree. As budgets tighten, prices rise, and information resources keep moving into a digital environment in which patron-driven access options naturally proliferate, it's quickly becoming harder for research libraries to justify the speculative building of just-in-case collections. This, as much as anything else, is what I believe is currently driving libraries away from time-honored models of traditional librarianship, and the repercussions of that shift are going to be as strong as they are unpredictable.

NOTES

1. Gary Rosen, "*Slander* by Ann Coulter," *Commentary* (November 2002): 81–86, www.commentarymagazine.com/articles/slander-by-ann-coulter.

2. See, for example, James Lindgren, "Fall from Grace: *Arming America* and the Bellesiles Scandal," *Yale Law Journal* 111 (2002): 2195–249, www.yalelawjournal.org/review/fall-from-grace-arming-america-and-the-bellesiles-scandal; and James Lindgren and Justin Heather, "Counting Guns in Early America," *William and Mary Law Review* 43 (2002): 1777–842, http://scholarship.law.wm.edu/cgi/viewcontent.cgi?article=1489&context=wmlr.

3. See, for example, the interview "In Depth with Garry Wills" on CSPAN's *BookTV* program, January 2, 2005, www.c-span.org/video/?184749-1/depth-garry-wills; see also comments attributed to Roger Lane in Jerome Sternstein's "Shooting the Messenger: Jon Weiner on *Arming America*," History News Network, August 8, 2005, http://historynewsnetwork.org/article/1074.

4. Allen Kent, *Use of Library Materials: The University of Pittsburgh Study* (New York: Marcel Dekker, 1979).

30

No, You May Not Come Train My Staff

IT'S BECOME A familiar ritual by now: several times during any given year—in fact, it happened again while I was writing this piece—a sales rep will call me on the phone or send me an e-mail with one of two apparently generous offers; he wants either (a) to come to my institution and meet with all the librarians in order to demonstrate the features and functionality of a new product, or (b) to come to my library and train my staff in the use of a database or e-journal package to which we already subscribe.

To both offers, I almost always say no.

Am I crazy? Why wouldn't I want to be informed about new and upcoming products that might be of use to my patrons? And don't we generally want vendors to offer us *more* training and product information rather than less?

Let me deal with those three questions one at a time.

Am I crazy?

I asked my wife to answer this one for me. She bit her lip and furrowed her brow silently for a moment, then asked me to define my terms. I withdrew the question.

Don't I want more training and product information?

Product information, yes.[1] If you're getting close to releasing a new product or service and you think it might be of interest to my institution, then please, by all means, tell me all about it. Ideally, I'd like you

---

This essay was originally published in *Against the Grain* 16, no. 4 (September 2004): 90.

to do so by means of a concise e-mail message with perhaps a one-page attachment (not a ten-page brochure) summarizing the product's purpose, characteristics, and pricing schedule. If I receive a message like that from you, and if I agree that the product on offer is something my institution should at least consider, I'll forward it to the appropriate people in my library and add it as an agenda item for discussion at our next collection development meeting. If I think it's something that clearly does not fit well with our needs or budget, I'll respond promptly and politely saying so. (If you bring up the same product in weekly e-mails over the course of the next month or two, however, my politeness will eventually start to deteriorate.)

If you must, you can call me on the phone instead of e-mailing the announcement to me. However, I probably won't be able to talk for very long, because if I'm near my phone, it's usually because I'm working, which means that I'll probably be in the middle of something when you call. And when the conversation is over, you're still going to have to send me an e-mail message with the product information attached; I'm not going to take notes from our conversation and then fashion them into a sales pitch to send to my colleagues on your behalf. You might as well save both of us some time and irritation by just sending me an e-mail to begin with.

So, yes, I'm happy to receive information about new products. However, I'm much less willing to gather our librarians together for a meeting with a sales rep for the purpose of hearing about a new product. Again, why? Don't I want my colleagues to know what's coming from our vendors? Don't I want to be notified when a product that may be of great interest to our patrons is about to be released? The answer is, yes, I do. But I'm only willing to pay a certain price for that information. If I gather forty full-time library employees for a one-hour meeting, it's as if I took one employee aside and said, "I want you to do nothing during this entire week but learn about Vendor X's new product." I do want to learn about the product, and I want my staff to learn about it as well, but I'd much rather get that information in a less thorough but (to me) completely acceptable format—e-mail—that will involve a relatively small investment of staff time. I understand why sales presentations are attractive to vendors' marketing departments: the rep has a captive audience, can control the presentation, and can influence the content of the discussion. But none of these benefits is very compelling from the library side. Yes, there are times (such as when we must decide between two expensive and competing online products or when we're establishing a new relationship or setting up a major new service with a vendor) when we do invite vendors to come and make presentations on-site. But in most cases, such visits are a very inefficient way for my staff and me to gather product information.

How about when you're designing a new product and want our input? Shouldn't we *want* to help ensure that these products will meet our patrons' needs rather than staying aloof from the design process and then complaining about the products' shortcomings after they're released? The answer to this question is another question: Yes, we're interested in helping, but why should our institution pay for the privilege? If you want the benefit of our expertise—in other words, if you want to use my library staff as an extension of your marketing department or your research and development group—then it should be you (not my institution) who pays for that time. At the institution where I work, my colleagues and I are available to provide consulting services at very reasonable fees.

Don't I want training in use of the vendor's products?

Short answer: no. Medium-length answer: if your product is so poorly designed that it takes an hour to train someone how to use it, then it's your product—not your customers—that needs fixing.

Long answer: My library serves a student population of about 30,000 and a faculty of about 2,500. You can come in and train my staff and me, but there is absolutely no way for us to pass that training on to more than a tiny fraction of those on our campus who will be using your product. Yes, we'll be able to train a few of them, but if we're paying a lot of money for your product (which is obviously the case, since you're willing to send a trainer to our campus), then a few isn't enough. We want *all* of our patrons to be able to use it with as little effort and confusion as possible. If you think about it, it's crazy to release a product to the market that is intended for unmediated use by inexperienced researchers but requires training before it can be used effectively. Sales reps are always shocked when I say no to such offers. I'm always shocked that they think the offer makes any kind of sense.

Now, I'm not saying that on-site training is always a bad idea. One thing that we do always want in our online products is a high level of administrative flexibility, and that usually comes at the cost of behind-the-scenes complexity. A product may have an exquisitely clean and intuitive user interface but a very complicated administrative module. Where such is the case, it can make very good sense to send us a rep who can train the staff members who will be using those functions. In such cases, the time invested by both parties in training is much more likely to return solid benefits to the product's users.

In all of the above, I hope I haven't come across as arrogant or ungrateful to those vendors and publishers who offer to send reps to my campus to inform us about new products or give us training. I realize that it costs vendors a lot of time and money to supply those services, and that they often do so in the belief that it's what their customers want and need. In fact, many have probably gotten requests for such visits from their library customers and may now be understandably frustrated to have another librarian saying that those visits are a big waste of time. To those vendors and publishers, all I can say is that attitudes on this issue will, obviously, differ widely from librarian to librarian. But in this, as in all other issues related to library work, we need to make sure that we're looking rigorously at the costs and benefits of our standard practices. Some practices that have become standard or automatic are no longer the best options available.

NOTE

1.   For discussion of this principle in the context of pricing models, see essay 26 in this volume.

31

On the Likelihood of Academia "Taking Back" Scholarly Publishing

IN ESSAY 24 of this volume, I discuss what I believe to be "signal distortions" contributing to a very weird set of economic dynamics in the scholarly publishing industry. At the end of that piece, I mention that there are some who would clearly welcome the "taking back" of scholarly publishing by the academy, and I promise to share thoughts about that.

The question I'd like to address here is not whether we in the academy should "take back publishing" from the commercial scholarly publishers but, rather, what the options for doing so might be, and whether any of those options seems feasible at the moment.

In considering this possibility, it seems to me that the first question we need to address is this: Would academia take back scholarly publishing by competing with traditional publishers (i.e., doing it *better than* publishers do it) or would we actually exclude commercial publishers from operating in the academic marketplace—saying, in essence, that there is no longer a legitimate marketplace for commercial publishing of academic work (i.e., doing it *instead of* letting publishers do it)?

Doing It Better: The Replicative Option

The competitive approach is, I believe, a real option. Scholarly publishing based in libraries or in university departments or colleges would not have to look exactly like traditional publishing, as long as it continues to provide authors those services that they demonstrably value

---

This essay was originally published in *The Scholarly Kitchen* (blog), June 27, 2013.

(review, editing, certification, dissemination, and archiving) as well as the things that readers demonstrably value (quality signaling and access). A non-commercial, academically based system could succeed as long as authors and readers both feel that it does all of those things, and does them as well as traditional publishing does, and as long as sufficient funding is provided to support it.

This road would itself require us to choose between two general strategies: either replicate all of the value-adds currently offered by traditional publishers (while perhaps adding some new ones as well) or decide to forego some of them—either because we don't actually agree that they provide value or because we don't feel the value they provide is worth the cost. Replicating them would be simpler in that it would not require both creating and building consensus around the acceptability of an entirely new system, but it would be more difficult in that it would require members of the academic community to take on all the roles and duties that commercial publishers fulfill under the current system. Those roles and duties have been effectively outsourced to the commercial marketplace for centuries; bringing them under the canopy of the academy, while certainly possible, would represent an enormous undertaking. More about this in a moment.

Doing It Instead: The Coercive Option

The exclusion option would be difficult if not impossible. To prohibit firms from participating commercially in the scholarly communication economy would require either that all scholars and scholarly institutions independently reach the same decision not to participate in commercial scholarly publishing (not terribly likely) or that they agree among themselves to unite to keep commercial publishers out of the system (which is also extremely unlikely and could constitute illegal collusion).

Another path to the exclusion option would be for government to legislate it. The law could theoretically prohibit commercial publishers from being involved in scholarly communication, though such legislation would probably have to apply only to works based on publicly funded scholarship. The emergence of such legal restriction seems unlikely for a variety of reasons, including:

- Laws that constrain publishing options would be somewhat at odds with free-speech protections.
- There is a strong tradition in academia of authors retaining control over their written work (despite its having been produced while in the employ of an institution).

- Providing separate systems for the publication of publicly and privately funded research results would be unwieldy and probably highly unpopular.
- Many scholarly authors (rightly or wrongly) have no quarrel with the existing system and would see little point in altering it so fundamentally.

The Real Monopolists

Those who bemoan the system under which knowledge is controlled monopolistically by publishers are objecting—whether they know it or not—to a system in which monopoly control is enjoyed first of all by the author. The current system is one in which authors generally trade monopoly control of their work for the prestige and added value that come from formal publication. Excluding commercial publishers from the academic marketplace would mean taking away the scholar's right to decide where he or she will publish. Scholars tend not to support systems that take away that right, which is why so many institutional open-access policies (in the United States, anyway) are not mandates in fact but, rather, statements of organizational preference.

Funder mandates have more coercive power, of course, and represent a third option that seems slowly to be gaining ground. But mandates such as those put in place at the National Institutes of Health and other federal granting agencies do not represent any transfer of power or control to the academy—in fact, just the opposite.

The Real Barrier

If we take it as given that of the three options outlined above—replicating, foregoing, and excluding—the one most likely to be accepted by authors is replication, then the question that remains is not whether academia could do it (the answer is almost certainly yes, given the will to redirect significant labor and funding from other endeavors) but whether there is any reason to believe that academia is likely to do so at the current scale, absent coercion. To my mind, the real barrier to academia "taking back publishing" is the simple fact that academics are already quite fully employed and it's not at all clear that a critical mass of them considers the existing system to be so broken that they would be willing to redirect significant resources to in-sourcing the functions currently fulfilled by commercial publishers.

There are libraries, departments, and other academic units publishing journals now, of course, and I think that's a healthy development. But not very many are doing so, and to my knowledge, no academic unit is publishing scores or hundreds of journals the way quite a few publishers do. In order to do so, they would have to take significant resources away from other important functions, many of which are likely more important in the minds of academics than radically changing the world of publishing is. On the other hand, it's true that there are many, many more academic units in the world than there are publishers, which means that no individual department would have to publish as many journals as, say, Wiley does in order for the system to continue at scale.

But maybe the current scale of publication isn't worth preserving. Is it possible we just don't need as many journals as we currently have? This proposition is somewhat belied by the constant growth in submissions that scholarly and scientific publishers report every year. Clearly, more and more research is being done, and more and more articles are seeking a home. While meeting that demand wouldn't have to mean a constant proliferation of journal *titles*—after all, *PLOS ONE* published more than 30,000 papers by itself in 2014—it would certainly require some other highly scalable solution, and the idea of any individual academic unit taking on a publishing project on the scale of *PLOS ONE* seems pretty silly.

What does this boil down to? My sense is that, for better or worse, we are unlikely to see a major shift in academic journal publishing out of the commercial sector and into the academic one anytime soon—not because there aren't downsides to the existing system, but because those who are freest to make meaningful decisions (authors and publishers) are the ones least likely to find fault with things as they are now and unlikely to see great value in either taking on (authors) or giving up (publishers) the roles that have accrued to them over the past few centuries. I may well be wrong. I guess we'll see.

32

Is a Rational Discussion of Open Access Possible?

Cost and Who Bears It

LET US BEGIN with the fundamental problem: scholarly information costs money. It costs money to generate information by doing research; having done the research, it then costs money to turn the results into a publishable document; having turned the results into a publishable document, it then costs money to make the document available to the world and to keep it that way.

Typically, the initial costs of *doing research* are borne by a combination of funding agencies and academic institutions. In the past, the costs of *turning research results into publishable documents* have been borne by a combination of academic institutions and publishers, while the costs of *making the documents available to the world* have initially been borne by publishers. Each of these three entities (funding agencies, academic institutions, and publishers) is funded from a different pool, though there is some overlap between them: public granting agencies are supported by tax revenues; private ones have their own endowments; academic institutions are funded by a combination of taxes, tuition, donations, commercialization revenue, and grants; publishers are usually supported by charging readers (or readers' agents, usually libraries) for access to the documents they publish.

This essay was originally presented as a lecture at the Smithsonian Libraries, March 10, 2014.

Economic and Philosophical Problems

No one much objects to funding agencies being underwritten by tax dollars or to universities being funded by taxes and tuition. But publishers charging for access to formally published scholarship is increasingly controversial for two reasons—one of them economic and one of them philosophical.

The economic consideration arises from aggressive pricing behavior on the part of many commercial scholarly publishers (and some putatively non-profit publishers as well) combined with relatively stagnant library budgets.[1] With journal prices continuing steadily to rise and with library budgets rising modestly if at all, there is a slow-motion crisis under way in the world of journal subscriptions. Regardless of one's philosophical view of the current publishing system, the economic problem of mismatch between prices and budgets is a real and pressing one.

The philosophical consideration arises largely from the fact that the content being sold to libraries by publishers originates in the very institutions to which it is being sold. Furthermore, not only are academic institutions producing the raw content, but they are providing much of the peer review and editorial work as well, usually without any compensation from the publishers to whom those services are provided; academics generally consider these services to be part of their contribution to the profession, and they do the work on university time. The idea of then paying what are, in some cases, extortionate prices for access to the fruits of this work is increasingly distasteful to many on the academic side.

The combination of concrete fiscal pressure and a mounting resentment toward publishers who take scholarly content out of academia and then sell it back to academia at a high price has led to the growth of the open-access (OA) movement, which proposes to make published scholarship freely available to the world.[2] This movement has arisen, not only because the current system is arguably unsustainable fiscally, but also from the feeling that it is morally indefensible—that it is simply wrong to deny people access to scholarship, especially when the public has underwritten the research from which it originates.[3]

Dissemination and Publishing

Now, let us look again at the four-part problem outlined above: it costs money to perform research, it costs money to turn research results into a publishable scholarly document, and it then costs money to make the document available to the world and to archive it permanently.

The third statement in that sequence is actually much less true than it used to be, because with the advent of the World Wide Web (and, more particularly, with the emergence of free blogging platforms), the cost of simply disseminating one's research results is now negligible. Today, any scholar who wants to bypass the formal publication system and make his findings freely available to the whole world can do so at essentially no cost either to himself or to his readers.

So if dissemination is essentially cost-free, why have traditional publishers survived? Why do scholars—who presumably want readership more than anything else, so that their ideas and discoveries can have an impact on their disciplines and bring recognition both to themselves and their institutions—willingly feed their manuscripts into a system that slows down the process of dissemination and then restricts access to those papers, letting them be read only by those who can pay for the privilege or who work at institutions that pay on their behalf?

One answer is that scholars do not, in fact, typically want maximum readership above all else. Scholarly communication is about much more than just telling the world what one has thought and discovered. It is also about review and certification. Telling the world that one has discovered a cure for cancer is easy, Google the phrase "cancer cure" and you will find a thousand people making just that claim. What is harder—what scholars and scientists want, and what costs money—is the process of taking submission of those claims, weeding out the obvious nonsense, subjecting the remainder to coordinated review, editing and formatting the papers that make it through that review, making them available, and creating and maintaining a robust and well-organized archive of them. Authors want that process to exist because when their work makes it through the process, it signals to their peers that the work is solid scholarship and should be taken seriously. Any model that proposes to do some or all of these things and then give the resulting documents to readers at no charge faces a problem: it will have to get financial support from a source other than readers.

I mentioned earlier that academia underwrites some parts of this process, because the editors of scholarly journals and the peer reviewers who provide first- or second-pass filtering of submissions are very often academics themselves, whose time is paid for by their host universities rather than by publishers. However, it is also true that their contribution to the scholarly certification process accounts for only some of the work and the cost that go into that process. Substantial costs are still borne by publishers as well.

The basic challenge, then, is this: the costs of producing scholarship have traditionally been underwritten partly by subsidies of academic time and effort, and partly by access fees paid by libraries and readers. To make scholarship freely available to readers threatens the viability of scholarly publishers, a few of which are large and very profitable multinational corporations, but most of which are non-profit professional and learned societies that regard publishing as a core element of their missions and depend on publishing revenue to underwrite services for their members.

Open-access models vary in their responses to this challenge, which is to be expected. What is distressing is what seems to me a tendency, particularly among the most prominent voices in the OA community, to insist that discussion of these models focus exclusively on their benefits, and to discourage and punish any discussion of their costs and downsides.

Let us look at those two statements separately.

The Open-Access Proposition: Benefits and Costs

First, in regard to the statement that OA models vary in their response to the cost challenge: The two broad models currently most prevalent are generally referred to as "Gold" and "Green."[4] Under the Gold model, formally published articles are made freely available to the public immediately upon publication, and the publisher's revenue stream is usually preserved either by some form of institutional subsidy or by payments exacted from authors. Under the Green model, articles are published as usual in toll-access journals; however, some version of each article (often the final peer-reviewed manuscript) is archived in a repository and made available to the general public. In many cases, an embargo period of six or twelve months is imposed on access to the deposited article in order to protect at least some of the publisher's ability to sell access to the formally published version.

Each of these models addresses the fiscal challenge in a different way. Each involves costs and benefits, and each of them entails consequences both intended and unintended.

An important, positive, and intended consequence of Gold OA is free public access to high-quality scholarly information. Another important (though unintended) consequence of the Gold model lies in the fact that since it provides for immediate free access, the publisher's incentive to maintain a high quality of output is weakened. This is not to say it disappears entirely or that Gold OA journals are necessarily of low quality—their quality, like that of toll-access journals, varies considerably. It is only to point out that when a business model does not rely on people buying the product, the incentive to invest in high quality is relatively weak. This is a problem when the journal in question is supported by institutional subsidy—but when a Gold OA journal is funded by author payments, the incentive problem becomes far worse. In fact, with an author-pays model, the quality incentives move from weak to actively perverse: if one's revenue increases with a higher rate of acceptance, then there is a strong incentive to accept papers without regard to quality. The implications of this perverse incentive are serious and are playing out with the emergence of what has come to be called "predatory publishing."[5]

Another downside to the author-pays version of Gold OA lies in the fact that authors do not typically pay these fees themselves but instead very often write them into research grant proposals. This means that funds are directed away from the support of new research and toward the free dissemination of prior research results. When OA journals are supported by institutional subventions, then the problem is one of opportunity cost: What must the organization stop doing in order to support an OA journal?

As for Green OA, an important, positive, and intended consequence of that model is free public access to high-quality scholarship. Another important (and at least partly unintended) consequence of this model is that it undermines the ability of publishers to recoup the investments they make in selecting and preparing articles for publication and in maintaining an ongoing archive of them afterward. In the case of this model, the perverse incentive lies, not with publishers, but with those who encourage and facilitate the model itself. Green OA relies on publishers continuing to add value to raw manuscripts and on readers and librarians continuing to buy subscriptions, but by making the resulting articles available for free, it reduces the subscribers' incentive to continue paying for them; this threatens to put publishers out of business and thus to undermine the Green OA model itself. Green OA can succeed in the long run only if it works poorly—if the versions available for free are substantially inferior to the versions available at a cost or if they are hard to find. If the model works so well that it results in universal, easy, immediate, and comprehensive access to high-quality articles at no cost, the incentive to pay for access disappears completely—and so, eventually, do the publishers on whom the model depends.

In summary, then, the OA movement has responded to genuine problems in the scholarly communication marketplace with a variety of strategies, each of which offers a mix of both very real benefits and advantages and very real costs and disadvantages.

Punishing Dissent

It has always seemed to me that the costs, benefits, merits, challenges, implications, and consequences of any dissemination model can (and should) be assessed and analyzed with some degree of dispassion and objectivity. This brings us to the second statement made above—the one concerning an unwillingness in the OA advocacy community to discuss (or even to countenance discussion of) these issues in that manner. The remainder of this essay will discuss manifestations of that unwillingness and propose steps that might be taken by those of us in the scholarly community who wish to encourage a more rational and inclusive discussion of these issues.

Some will be tempted to dismiss what I say on this topic out of hand because I write for *The Scholarly Kitchen*, a professional blog where scholarly communication issues (including OA) are discussed in a critical mode, and which is often characterized by OA advocates as an anti-OA forum. This is an unfortunate but common response, and it illustrates the problem I will describe.[6]

For example, in early 2014, I published a posting in *The Scholarly Kitchen* blog that pointed out some serious problems with ROAR-MAP, an influential registry that claimed, misleadingly, to be a registry of "mandatory archiving policies."[7] One OA advocate, instead of addressing the pervasive errors and misinformation documented in my posting, responded (via Twitter) simply by asserting ROARMAP's wonderfulness and attacking *The Scholarly Kitchen* for talking about ROARMAP's problems. This was only one response, of course, but similar reactions from others are documented in the comments section of the posting. Another response, on the blog of influential OA advocate Stevan Harnad, questioned my motives in drawing attention to the problem, characterizing *The Scholarly Kitchen* posting as "skulduggery" and referring to the blog as the "Scholarly Scullery."[8] None of this constitutes rational discussion; it is an attempt to avoid it.

The ROARMAP site itself also provides an example of the dynamic in question: instead of accurately and objectively presenting data about institutional OA policies, it presents such data inaccurately and in a manner that seems, in this author's opinion, clearly designed to exaggerate those aspects of the policies that the site's owners find most congenial. Nor is ROARMAP the only such example: the MELIBEA registry, based in Barcelona, is, if anything, less accurate than ROARMAP in its presentation of OA policies, as demonstrated in the subsequent discussion in *The Scholarly Kitchen*.[9]

Much of the controversy about these registries arises from the strange insistence, on the part of some prominent members of the OA community, on referring to all OA policies as "mandates," even if they have nothing mandatory about them. I asked two of the people responsible for ROARMAP why the systematic exaggeration is necessary.

One (according to Harnad) chose not to respond because I write for *The Scholarly Kitchen*. The other—Harnad himself—responded (in the comments section of *The Scholarly Kitchen* posting cited above) by simply repeating, at length, the assertion that all OA policies should be called "mandates" regardless of whether they are mandatory, and by speculating once more about whose interests I was trying to serve by raising the issue. This, again, is not rational discussion; it is an attempt to shout down and discredit the messenger.[10]

Strategic Overreaction and Willful Ignorance

A related tendency among OA advocates might be called "strategic overreaction." In 2013, the American Historical Association called on institutions to allow graduate students to embargo their dissertations for up to six years (instead of the two or three typically allowed now).[11] This was characterized by OA supporters on Twitter as "shocking" and "repressive"; a scholar who tweeted his support for the AHA's position was publicly characterized as "dumb as a box of hair." One librarian who took exception to the AHA's statement characterized it, sneeringly, as a call to "protect the children" and to "turn the clock back."[12] Fair enough; this is the Internet, after all, and there is nothing wrong with expressing one's opinion, however over-the-top it may seem. What undermines rational discourse more seriously, however, is when one criticizes a statement that one has not made a good-faith attempt to understand or even to read. In this case, many of the AHA's harshest critics seem actually not to have read the statement, since a good number of them characterized it as a call for embargoes, which it clearly and explicitly was not—it was a call for authors to be allowed to embargo their dissertations for a longer period than usual, if they so choose. One critic who did read the statement and saw how uncontroversial its actual content was chose, therefore, to criticize the statement's "subtext" instead of its text—or, in other words, to take it to task for things it did not say but which the critic was sure it really meant.[13] It does not seem to me that name-calling, misrepresentation, and mind-reading are examples of rational discussion. Instead, they are attempts to avoid and derail it.

The most egregious example of this kind of reaction, however, came in response to science journalist John Bohannon's study of editorial practices at several hundred OA journals.[14] He orchestrated a sort of sting operation, whereby he submitted a putatively scholarly paper (which actually contained nothing but nonsense) to 304 author-pays OA journals, just over half of which accepted it for publication. His finding reflects the perverse incentive discussed above: a journal that makes its money by accepting papers rather than by selling access to high-quality content has a natural incentive to accept low-quality papers. Instead of acknowledging this problem and expressing concern over the degree to which it is reflected in the practices of quite a few OA journals—practices that Bohannon demonstrated conclusively—the OA community generally responded by attacking Bohannon.[15] Now to be clear, Bohannon's investigation was not perfect and there are legitimate criticisms to be made of it; what is not in question, though, is that he identified a large population of OA journals that are willing to accept nonsense in return for payment and then present it to the world as science. The OA community's defensive response suggests a widespread unwillingness to discuss or even acknowledge—let alone deal with—this problem.[16]

Shooting the Messenger and Magical Thinking

What all of this means, I believe, is that OA's growth and progress are being hampered by a "shoot the messenger" culture that inhibits the OA community's ability to deal with real issues and challenges. The only challenges that are allowed to be discussed are those related to how best to spread the word of OA, how to implement OA programs, and how to achieve maximum adoption of OA policies. Challenges and problems that *arise from OA itself* are not to be discussed; attempts to discuss them are punished.

There is another aspect to this problem, though, and it has less to do with attacking those who raise questions or concerns than it does with trying to prevent or pre-empt concerns from being expressed in the first place. Two strategies are widely employed in this regard: the first is to talk constantly about OA's inevitability, its inexorable rise, its dramatic and unstoppable growth, and so forth, in terms that have more in common with war propaganda than with rational discourse.[17] This tendency can sometimes be a bit embarrassing, but it is not terribly serious—flag-waving has its place, after all. More troublesome is a second strategy, which is to encourage OA advocates to pretend that the war is already won. Consider this quote from a prominent American OA leader and lobbyist (emphasis in the original):

> I think it is critical for us to recognize that the moment is in our hands when we need to stop thinking of Open Access as fighting to *become* the norm for research and scholarship, and to begin acting in ways that acknowledge that Open Access *is* the norm.[18]

Such language represents, not a call for rational discourse, but a call for magical thinking. Responsible estimates of OA's penetration of scholarly publishing currently range from 2.5 percent of articles (under Gold and hybrid models) to 20 percent (under Gold and Green combined), but even at the top end, it is quite clear that toll-access models remain very much the norm in scholarly publishing.[19] Pretending otherwise might be inspiring, but it undermines our ability to talk in useful and realistic ways about the challenges that exist in the real world. More perniciously, it also erodes our motivation to address real problems created by OA initiatives; after all, if OA has already conquered the world of scholarly publishing, what point is there in raising concerns about it or pointing out problems?

Another example of magical thinking is the common assertion that in cases where the public has paid for research, this means the public has paid for the articles that result from it. This argument is implied in common phrases like "taxpayer access to publicly funded research." It uses a word game to produce an economic sleight-of-hand illusion: by pretending that the terms "research" and "article" mean the same thing, one can hide the significant costs involved in turning research results into articles. In reality, however, what the public usually funds is some combination of the research itself and the initial writing up of its results, not the costly and subsequent processes that turn research results into finished and edited documents that can be accessed by the public.[20] (One might as well argue that since the public paid for the subway to be built, no one should have to pay to ride it.)

What about OA opponents? Are they more willing to discuss these matters in a reasonable way? In fairness, I obviously have to address this question. The problem is, it is difficult to think of anyone who, to my knowledge, actually opposes OA (other than, perhaps, Jeffrey Beall, who has done excellent work on the problem of predatory publishing but whose recent article attacking the OA movement was, in my view, unbalanced, inaccurate, and unfair.[21]) Even my fellow writers in *The*

Scholarly Kitchen—despite the way we are regularly characterized in the OA blogosphere—are not generally opposed to it; several of us (myself included), in fact, are actively involved in supporting OA programs. In my experience, a person will be characterized as an enemy not for actually opposing OA but, rather, for making any public suggestion that OA entails problems and costs as well as benefits.

Now, it is important to note that some organizations—particularly organizations of publishers and authors, such as the DC Principles Coalition, the Association of American Publishers, and the Copyright Alliance—do sometimes oppose particular OA initiatives, and some have taken an organizational stance that is more or less generally anti-OA.[22] However, none of these organizations or their representatives have, to my knowledge, engaged in the kind of shaming and conversation-stopping behaviors that I see regularly on the advocacy side.

Advocacy vs. Analysis

What we need is an environment in which it is possible for all stakeholders to speak openly, candidly, and rationally about the pros and cons, the costs and benefits, of all publishing models—not without fear of contradiction, but without being shamed, silenced, or accused of bad faith simply for raising important and troublesome issues. When discussing OA, we must be able to talk about both its benefits and its costs, because when we insist on talking only about benefits, we are engaging not in analysis but in advocacy. Advocacy has its place, but its limitations should be obvious: it is in the nature of advocacy to try to quash any suggestion that the thing for which one is advocating produces anything other than benefits. This seriously limits the advocate's ability to deal in a reasonable and effective way with real-world problems.[23]

The irony is that when a community of practice pushes analysis aside in favor of advocacy, it reduces its own effectiveness as a community. Advocacy is actively counterproductive if it means actively discouraging the discussion of real issues and problems. One can ignore reality for only so long before it finally wins. To be clear, none of this is to say that anyone should stop advocating for OA. What I do hope is that those who do so will refrain from demonizing, misrepresenting, and silencing those who try to discuss OA in a spirit of critical analysis.

It is important to point out that not everyone working for open access is trying to silence dissenters and doubters—but the voices trying to discourage discussion and debate, and to shame anyone who raises concerns, are loud and public, and I would be much less concerned about that if I saw more prominent figures in the movement standing up publicly in favor of open debate and critical analysis. There are many voices in the OA community calling on us to fall into line, to come to the altar, and to accept either that resistance is futile or that victory is inevitable (depending on one's perspective). I wish there were more voices inviting us to raise concerns, to help identify and resolve issues, and to anticipate problems. I wish I saw the embrace of dissent that most of us in libraries would, in any other context, consider to be an essential aspect of intellectual engagement. Some skeptics are willing to raise their voices even if by doing so they run the risk of being put on an enemies list, but too many others have decided that keeping their heads down is the better and safer path.[24] The sad thing is that the OA community would almost certainly benefit, in the long run, from listening to what the critics and questioners have to say.

What Is to Be Done?

How, then, do we foster an environment in which critical and constructive discussion of OA is possible? Here are six steps that I believe all of us—no matter where we sit on the advocacy spectrum—can take:

Acknowledge that all models have pros and cons. Any discussion that proceeds from the assumption that open access (or toll access or any other model of scholarly communication) has only upsides or only downsides is a discussion that will not be honest and is highly unlikely to be rational and productive. Even a system that produces universal access to scholarship will have downsides that impact dimensions of scholarship other than access. Here is a thought experiment that each of us can undertake in the privacy of our own minds: Think of your favorite access model. Perhaps you are a commercial publisher and subscription revenues are essential to your business; maybe you are an OA advocate and your ideal scenario is universal and immediate Green OA. Ask yourself this question: "If my ideal solution were universally adopted, what would be the downsides for scholarship?" If you can think of none, then one of two things is true: either your preferred model is perfect or you are not examining your model fairly.

Comprehend, and then respond. Too often, productive conversation is derailed because one or more of the participants is responding not to what was said but to some distortion or misrepresentation of what was said. Each of us can be careful to avoid that mistake and can quickly take responsibility when we do make it.

Focus on the substance of statements, not on the supposed motivations of the speaker. It is a difficult and unpleasant fact, but a fact nevertheless, that a miserable person of ill will can speak the truth. While the speaker's intent is not entirely irrelevant, when it comes to finding workable solutions to real-world problems, it is ultimately the truth or untruth of a proposition that matters most. Attributing ill intent to others is, far too often, a ploy for distracting people from the substantive issue.

Avoid "poisoned well" and ad hominem arguments. This is related to the question of motivation, but it is not quite the same thing. Poisoned well and ad hominem arguments say, "No matter what that person says, we should not listen because he is a bad person or believes in Bad Thing X." Anytime one encounters this line of argument, it is very likely that the person making it is afraid of what will happen if one looks closely at the issue in question and is therefore trying to shift the focus away from the issue and toward the defects of the person raising it. None of us should engage in this kind of argumentation.

Take unintended and unexpected consequences seriously. No matter what initiative one undertakes—a new toll-access journal, an open-access policy, an institutional repository, a change in copyright law—some of the consequences of that initiative will be intended and wished for and others will be unexpected and undesired. One of the dangers of advocacy is that it carries with it an incentive to discount the unintended and the unexpected and to focus on the intended and the expected. Advocacy leads us to emphasize convenient truths and either to deny or to downplay inconvenient ones. Again: this is not to say that there is no place for advocacy in the conversation about OA—only that we need to be aware of its limitations as a frame for useful and responsible discussion.

Invite all stakeholders to the table. I will close by sharing a quote from my colleague T. Scott Plutchak, Director of the Lister Hill Library at the University of Alabama—and, for the record, an OA supporter. A few years ago, Scott participated in a Scholarly Publishing Roundtable that was convened by the US Congress under the aegis of the House Science and Technology Committee. The roundtable included representatives from both the public and the private sectors, including librarians, scholars, academic administrators, toll-access publishers, OA publishers, and scholarly society officers. The documents and recommendations resulting from the group's work can be found on the Association of American Universities' website, and they are very interesting; one outcome worth noting is that two members of the group (one from a large commercial science publisher and another from a large non-profit OA publisher) chose formally not to endorse its findings.[25] Plutchak later observed (emphasis added):

[T]he recommendations of the Roundtable . . . were largely incorporated into the America COMPETES Act and substantially informed the requirements laid out in the Holdren OSTP memo. The Roundtable remains, as far as I'm aware, the only significant OA-related activity to have active and equal participation from librarians, publishers large and small, commercial and not-for-profit, as well as senior representatives from the university community. Certainly *its success in influencing federal policy is a reflection of that, despite the fact that it was that very inclusiveness that led to its being immediately dismissed by many of the loud voices in the debate.* It has been explicit in our discussions with policy makers that they are seeking moderate and inclusive views to help develop policy.[26]

Moderation and inclusiveness are unpopular notions in many segments of our society today, and nowhere more so, I believe, than in the scholarly communication wars. The problem is that when we are dealing with complex problems involving many stakeholders, needs that are in tension with each other, and inevitable trade-offs, moderation and inclusiveness are essential to a rational and productive discussion.

NOTES

1. Steven Bosch and Kittie Henderson, "Steps Down the Evolutionary Road: Periodicals Price Survey 2014," *Library Journal* 139 (April 2014): 32–37.

2. Peter Suber, "A Very Brief Introduction to Open Access" (published online December 29, 2004), http://legacy.earlham.edu/~peters/fos/brief.htm.

3. Philip Young, "The Serials Crisis and Open Access: A White Paper for the Virginia Tech Commission on Research" (unpublished report, 2009), http://eprints.rclis.org/14118; SPARC, "Open Access," http://sparc.arl.org/issues/open-access.

4. Stevan Harnad et al., "The Access/Impact Problem and the Green and Gold Roads to Open Access," *Serials Review* 30, no. 4 (2004): 310–14.

5. Jeffrey Beall, *Scholarly Open Access—Critical analysis of scholarly open-access publishing* (blog), http://scholarlyoa.com.

6. Screenshot illustrations of many of the examples provided in the following text can be found, alongside a full transcript of the lecture upon which this essay is based, at http://discussingoa.wordpress.com.

7. Rick Anderson, "Errors and Misinformation in the ROARMAP Open Access Registry," *The Scholarly Kitchen* (blog), February 13, 2014, http://scholarlykitchen.sspnet.org/2014/02/13/errors-and-misinformation-in-

the-roarmap-open-access-registry; ROARMAP—Registry of Open Access Repositories Mandatory Archiving Policies (now called Registry of Open Access Repository Mandates and Policies), http://roarmap.eprints.org.

8. Stevan Harnad, "More Skulduggery from SSP's Scholarly Scullery," *Open Access Archivangelism* (blog), February 15, 2014, http://openaccess. eprints.org/index.php?/archives/1098-More-Skulduggery-from-SSPs-Scholarly-Scullery.html.

9. MELIBEA—Directory and estimator policies for open access to scientific production, www.accesoabierto.net/politicas/?idioma=en.

10. It should be noted that within months of my *Scholarly Kitchen* posting about ROARMAP, its owners took steps that greatly improved its reliability and accuracy.

11. American Historical Association, "American Historical Association Statement on Policies Regarding the Embargoing of Completed History PhD Dissertations," *AHA Today* (blog), July 22, 2013, http://j. mp/19dVi5h.

12. Barbara Fister, "The AHA Asks 'What about the Children?,'" *Library Babel Fish* (blog), July 24, 2013, www.insidehighered.com/blogs/library-babel-fish/aha-asks-what-about-children#sthash.uA1BGgZu.dpbs.

13. Brian Sarnacki, "The Ivoriest Tower" (July 26, 2013), www.briansarnacki. com/the-ivoriest-tower/.

14. John Bohannon, "Who's Afraid of Peer Review?," *Science* 342 (2013): 60–65.

15. See, for example: The Library Loon, "Which Is It?," *Gavia Libraria* (blog), October 3, 2013, http://gavialib.com/2013/10/which-is-it; Mike Taylor, "Anti-tutorial: How to Design and Execute a Really Bad Study," *SV-POW* (blog), October 7, 2013, http://svpow.com/2013/10/07/anti-tutorial-how-to-design-and-execute-a-really-bad-study; Bjorn Brembs, "How Embarrassing Was the 'Journal Sting' for Science Magazine?" (October 6, 2013), http://bjoern.brembs.net/2013/10/how-embarrassing-was-the-journal-sting-for-science-magazine. Shortly after publication of Bohannon's study, it was widely reported that the Directory of Open Access Journals had responded with accusations of racism, though the link to which all of these reports refer (http://doaj.org/doaj?func=news &nId=315&uiLanguage=en) is now dead. In contrast to these reactions, prominent OA advocate Peter Suber's analysis, though critical on balance, struck me as admirably honest and even-handed: Peter Suber, "New 'Sting' of Weak Open-Access Journals" (October 3, 2013), https:// plus.google.com/+PeterSuber/posts/CRHeCAtQqGq.

16. Though widespread, this unwillingness is not universal. The Open Access Scholarly Publishers Association, for example, has

acknowledged the problems raised by Bohannon's study and made a public commitment to tighten its membership criteria and exercise better oversight. (See Claire Redhead, "OASPA's Second Statement Following the Article in *Science* Entitled 'Who's Afraid of Peer Review?'" [November 11, 2013], http://oaspa.org/2013/11.) It has also been widely reported that the Directory of Open Access Journals removed 114 or more journals from its list in light of Bohannon's findings, though the DOAJ's statement to that effect seems no longer to be available online.

17.   David Lewis, "The Inevitability of Open Access," *College and Research Libraries* 73 (September 2012): 493–506; Stephen Curry, "The Inexorable Rise of Open Access Scientific Publishing," *Occam's Corner* (blog), *The Guardian*, October 22, 2012, www.theguardian.com/ science/occams-corner/2012/oct/22/inexorable-rise-open-access-scientific-publishing; Heather Morrison, "The Unstoppable Growth of High Quality Open Access Resources," *The Imaginary Journal of Poetic Economics* (blog), December 11, 2013, http://poeticeconomics. blogspot.ca/2013/12/the-unstoppable-growth-of-high-quality.html. When reading the public pronouncements of some OA advocates, one is constantly reminded of the government radio announcements in George Orwell's *1984*: "A news flash has this moment arrived from the Malabar front. Our forces in South India have won a glorious victory."

18.   Richard Poynder, "Heather Joseph on the State of Open Access: Where Are We, and What Needs to Be Done?," *Open and Shut?* (blog), July 12, 2013, http://poynder.blogspot.com/2013/07/heather-joseph-on-state-of-open-access.html.

19.   Richard Poynder, "Open Access by Numbers," *Open and Shut?* (blog), June 19, 2011, http://poynder.blogspot.com/2011/06/open-access-by-numbers.html; Bo-Christer Björk, Annikki Roos, and Mari Lauri, "Scientific Journal Publishing: Yearly Volume and Open Access Availability", *Information Research* 14, no. 1 (March 2009), www. informationr.net/ir/14-1/paper391.html.

20.   This issue is discussed in some depth in a debate between the author of the present essay and Jean-Claude Guédon of the University of Montréal; transcripts of their statements and responses can be found at http://2013charlestonconference.sched.org/event/c9cf410d4aef11f6e 305c8bbbbab713c#.U1AifNweEpo.

21.   Jeffrey Beall, "The Open-Access Movement Is Not Really about Open Access," *tripleC* 11 (2013): 589–97.

22.   See, for example: Washington DC Principles for Free Access to Science, "Nonprofit Publishers Oppose Government Mandates for Scholarly

Publishing" (press release, February 20, 2007), www.dcprinciples. org/press/2.htm; Association of American Publishers and the Washington DC Principles for Free Access to Science (untitled, joint letter to Congress opposing the Federal Research Public Access Act, July 30, 2009), www.dcprinciples.org/news/FRPAA.pdf); Peter Suber, "Copyright Alliance and AAP Welcome Re-introduction of Conyers Bill," *Open Access News* (blog), February 5, 2009, http://legacy.earlham. edu/~peters/fos/2009/02/copyright-alliance-and-aap-welcome-re.html. See also, for example: the Association of American Publishers' statement on open access at http://publishers.org/news/us-publishers-endorse-international-joint-statement-open-access-debate-0, and Washington DC Principles for Free Access to Science, "A Statement from Not-for-Profit Publishers" (March 16, 2004), www.dcprinciples.org/statement.htm. While neither statement is explicitly anti-OA, in both cases, the anti-OA message seems to me strongly implicit.

23. For further discussion of this issue, see essay 23 in this volume.

24. Stevan Harnad, "Is the Library Community Friend or Foe of OA?," *Open Access Archivangelism* (blog), September 16, 2013, http://openaccess. eprints.org/index.php?/archives/1051-Is-the-Library-Community-Friend-or-Foe-of-OA.html.

25. Association of American Universities, "Scholarly Publishing Roundtable," www.aau.edu/policy/scholarly_publishing_roundtable. aspx?id=6894; Y. S. Chi, "Comments of YS Chi to the 'Scholarly Publishing Roundtable' Delegates" (undated letter), www.aau.edu/ WorkArea/DownloadAsset.aspx?id=10054; Mark Patterson, "Statement from Mark Patterson: Why PLoS Has Not Signed the Report of the Scholarly Publishing Roundtable," (undated letter), www.aau.edu/ WorkArea/DownloadAsset.aspx?id=10050.

26. T. Scott Plutchak, comment (February 21, 2014) on Alice Meadows, "Collaborate, Co-operate, Communicate!," *The Scholarly Kitchen* (blog), February 20, 2014, http://scholarlykitchen.sspnet.org/2014/02/20/ open-access-why-it-needs-to-take-a-village.

33

CC BY, Copyright, and Stolen Advocacy

IN A 2014 *New York Times* story, journalist Denver David Robinson tells of how while working in Uganda for a non-profit organization, he did a photojournalism project for *The Advocate* magazine.[1] His project helped "a dozen members of the [LGBTQ] community [tell] their stories, most for the first time." The essay was published both online and in *The Advocate*'s February–March 2013 print issue.

One year later, Uganda's president signed into law the Anti-Homosexuality Act, making "sexual relations between persons of the same sex" a crime punishable by imprisonment and/or death.[2] (The law was annulled later that year.)

In the wake of that legislation's enactment, a Ugandan tabloid called *Red Pepper* reportedly published an article (which doesn't seem to be available online, thus sparing me having to decide whether to link to it) with the title "Homosexuality Could Cause Mental Illness—Medics." According to Robinson's report in *The New York Times*, the article included, without his permission, one of the copyrighted photos from his project.

It then gets worse. A few months later, the same tabloid published a version of Robinson's entire photo essay—again without his permission—with a new title ("Top Ugandan Gays Speak Out: How We Became Homos") and with Robinson's name, among others, in the byline. (In the wake of this unauthorized republication, *The Advocate* removed the online version of Robinson's original piece; its editor subsequently tried to contact those whose photos appeared in it to see whether they were still willing to be publicly identified as gay.)

This essay was originally published in *The Scholarly Kitchen* (blog), March 31, 2014.

Shortly thereafter, Robinson reported plans to file suit against *Red Pepper* in Uganda for copyright infringement.

Why am I writing about this in *The Scholarly Kitchen*? Because for some time I have been concerned with the growing movement to pressure scholarly authors into publishing their original work under a Creative Commons "Attribution" license (known for short as CC BY) rather than under the terms of traditional copyright. As explained at the Creative Commons website, CC BY licenses allow anyone to "distribute, remix, tweak, and build upon your work, even commercially, as long as they credit you for the original creation."[3] The pressure on authors to adopt CC BY takes a number of forms. Some definitions of open access (OA), including those of the Berlin Declaration and the Bethesda Statement, explicitly require, not just free public access to the document in question, but also public reuse rights that overlap significantly or completely with the terms of CC BY.[4] Membership in the Open Access Scholarly Publishers Association (OASPA) is also subject to this requirement.[5] The Scholarly Publishing and Academic Resources Coalition (SPARC) "considers the terms outlined by the . . . [CC BY license] to be the standard terms for Open Access."[6] The Wellcome Trust requires that all APC-funded OA articles resulting from research that it funds be published under CC BY.[7]

To be clear, there are many good things about CC BY and good reasons to adopt CC BY licensing in one's work, especially if one is a scholar or scientist, and I believe authors should have maximum freedom to publish under those terms if they so choose. But there can also be good reasons to hesitate, as Robinson's experience indicates. If you tell the world, "Use my work in any way you wish, just make sure you identify me as the author," you're authorizing not only responsible academic and professional reuse and distribution but also any other kinds of reuse that might fit an academic, social, or political agenda with which you do not wish to be associated. Because Robinson published his article under traditional copyright, he has legal recourse against those who have misappropriated his work; if he had published it under CC BY, he would have no recourse at all because, in publishing terms, the kind of reuse being made of his work is exactly what CC BY is designed to allow.

The *Red Pepper* case is obviously only tangentially related to academic publishing. But last year we saw a troubling (if less repugnant) example of how this can happen in the academic realm. Apple Academic Press published a book titled *Epigenetics, Environment, and Genes*. The book was comprised almost entirely of articles taken, without their authors' permission, from OA journals in which they had been published under CC BY licenses. As of this writing, it is available on Amazon at a list price of $129.95. Although members of the scholarly community have responded with outrage, Apple Academic Press has done nothing illegal or even unethical. As long as the authors of the articles are given due credit, this kind of reuse is one of the many that are explicitly allowed under CC BY. If the authors feel mistreated by Apple Academic, it's because they failed to read (or understand) the agreements they signed when they submitted their articles for publication in OA outlets. What is troubling about this example is not so much what the publisher did but the fact that authors are apparently being pushed to adopt CC BY licensing without understanding its ramifications. Ultimately, the responsibility for gaining that understanding lies with the authors, but this points up one more reason for all of us in the scholarly community to be as open and up front as possible about those ramifications as we discuss and debate policy initiatives.

Obviously, it needs to be said that traditional copyright doesn't strictly prevent people from appropriating your original work and reusing it for repulsive and hateful purposes, any more than laws against burglary have eradicated break-ins or laws against assault have resulted in a violence-free society. What copyright does do, however, is give the author legal recourse in the event that his or her work is appropriated and reused by others without permission and in ways to which the author objects. In the case of Denver David Robinson, he now has the option of filing suit against the publication that stole his work and perverted its intentions. It may or may not work—but if he had published his piece under a CC BY license, he would have no recourse at all. (The tabloid even gave him attribution, though in this situation that fact only made the situation more repugnant to the author.)

The more general issue here is not so much about the relative merits of copyright and CC BY licensing, however; it's about the Law of Unintended Consequences generally. We may undertake a project or a program with nothing but the best intentions, seeing all the ways in which it might make the world a better place. But, invariably, if the project or program is enacted, it will also have consequences we did not foresee (and in many cases could not have foreseen), and they will never be uniformly positive. When an author gives up the right to control republication and the creation of derivative works, she makes her original work much more available for positive reuse—but also for irresponsible or even hateful reuse, since she gives up the right to say how, where, whether, and in what context her work will be repurposed.

Authors who find this troubling are not being unreasonable. This is an issue that needs, I believe, wider and more rigorous discussion.

NOTES

1. Denver David Robinson, "The Ugandan Tabloid That Stole Our Pride," *The New York Times*, March 16, 2014: 23.

2. "The Anti Homosexuality Bill" (2009), http://bit.ly/1P14EJ6.

3. Creative Commons, "About the Licenses," http://creativecommons.org/licenses.

4. "Berlin Declaration on Open Access to Knowledge in the Sciences and Humanities" (October 22, 2003), http://openaccess.mpg.de/Berlin-Declaration; "Bethesda Statement on Open Access Publishing" (released June 20, 2003), http://legacy.earlham.edu/~peters/fos/bethesda.htm.

5. Claire Redhead, "Why CC BY?" (October 23, 2012), http://oaspa.org/why-cc-by.

6. SPARC, "Open Access," www.sparc.arl.org/issues/open-access.

7. Wellcome Trust, "Open Access: CC-BY Licence Required for All Articles Which Incur an Open Access Publication Fee—FAQ" (last updated August 2015), www.wellcome.ac.uk/stellent/groups/corporatesite/@policy_communications/documents/web_document/WTVM055715.pdf.

34

Open-Access Rhetoric, Economics, and the Definition of "Research"

I FIND MYSELF becoming increasingly troubled by the popular phrase "access to publicly funded research," which is commonly invoked by advocates of open-access (OA) solutions to the problem of access to scientific journal articles. Search Google for that phrase and you'll get hundreds of thousands of results: statements from the Alliance for Taxpayer Access ("American taxpayers are entitled to the research they've paid for"), the Organisation for Economic Co-operation and Development ("Governments should improve access to publicly funded research"), and the New York State Higher Education Initiative ("Support open access to public funded research"), among many others.[1]

But there's a serious problem with that phrase and its variants, popular as they may be. The problem is that it's misleading: there is no such thing as "access to research." Research is an activity in which scientists and scholars engage, not an object or product to which people can be given access. What those who invoke the phrase actually want is public access to the published (or at least peer-reviewed) versions of papers that result from publicly funded research. The latter, clunkier formulation exposes a reality that the former, sleeker one obscures: the large and expensive gap that lies between the completion of a scientific experiment (which is what funding agencies have historically provided funding for, and which is what is commonly meant by the term "research") and the creation of a publishable product based on that research.

Once the research has been done, two things have to happen in order to create the desired product: the resulting data has to be digested and

---

This essay was originally published as "OA Rhetoric, Economics, and the Definition of 'Research'" in *The Scholarly Kitchen* (blog), September 7, 2011.

turned into a document, and the document has to be edited and turned into something publishable. It's technically possible to bypass the second of those two processes, at least temporarily, and provide public access to a preliminary version of the research report; this happens every day on the arXiv, for example. But these are not the documents to which OA advocates want the public to have access. OA, whether Green or Gold, is about giving people free access to peer-reviewed research journal articles.

The processes of preparing research reports for publication and making the resulting documents available to readers cost money, of course, as does the process of keeping access available on an ongoing basis. None of those costs has traditionally been borne by the agencies that fund research; instead, they have usually been borne by subscribers to scientific journals. This arrangement has led to some severe problems, most notable among them the serials pricing crisis.[2] Quickly and relentlessly rising journal prices combined with stagnant or declining library budgets mean that libraries can provide less and less access to published content from year to year (despite the temporary and artificial economies afforded by models such as the Big Deal, which is manifestly unsustainable in the long run). This is a real and severe problem, and OA offers an obvious solution to it: once access is free, the serials crisis, or at least one manifestation of it, is solved.

However, a model under which the costs of editorial preparation, publication, and permanent maintenance are transferred from journal subscribers to funding agencies carries with it problems as well, and in my experience, OA advocates are often unwilling to entertain serious discussion of those problems.[3] One rhetorical mechanism for avoiding such discussion is the insistence that the costs of publication are inseparable from the costs of research.

One large funding agency, the Wellcome Trust, has in the past made this insistence a part of its public posture with the phrase "[We believe] that dissemination costs are research costs."[4] Other commentators have, somewhat amusingly, gone so far as to assert that unless a research paper has been formally published, the research has not happened. Jean-Claude Guédon is one of the more prominent OA advocates to take this stance; in a posting to the SCHOLCOMM LISTSERV on August 30, 2011, he asserted that "research without dissemination is not research," proceeding from that premise to the position that "hence, dissemination is an integral part of research and, therefore, of research costs."[5]

This statement is worth unpacking because if taken seriously by policymakers and funding agencies, it has serious implications both for access and for research itself.

There is a logical syllogism behind statements like "Dissemination costs are research costs" and "Research without dissemination is not research." The syllogism is as follows:

1. The public has provided funds for research.
2. Dissemination is an integral part of research.
   Therefore,
3. The public has funded dissemination.

The problem with this logic is (or ought to be) obvious: while one may play with the definition of "research" in whatever way one wishes, there is an intractable fiscal reality at work that remains unaffected by such word games, and that reality is that funding agencies have not traditionally funded "research" in this elastic, postmodern sense but, rather, "research" in the sense implied by both colloquial usage and most dictionary definitions—the systematic inquiry into a question or hypothesis. The production of an article after a research project is complete is not only conceptually separable from the research itself but, more importantly, involves costs that are subsequent and additional to the costs incurred by the research project. To argue that "dissemination costs are research costs" is to conflate the two categories of cost by means of rhetorical sleight-of-hand. It is also to smuggle a moral or "should" argument ("The public should not have to pay for access") inside the Trojan horse of a fallacious "is" statement ("The public has already paid for access, since dissemination is an integral part of research and the public paid for the research").

It is, of course, possible for funding agencies to underwrite the costs of dissemination as well as the costs of research itself. Some already do so; in 2014, the Wellcome Trust allocated just over $7 million to cover Gold OA charges, and in 2005 (the last time it attempted an estimate), the National Institutes of Health estimated that it "pays over $30 million annually in direct costs for publication and other page charges in grants to its investigators."[6] Thirty-seven million dollars is serious money, and it means a serious tradeoff: money that is redirected from the support of actual research to the underwriting of OA dissemination thereby becomes unavailable for the support of research projects. The result is both broader public access (clearly a very good thing) and fewer research findings (a potentially very bad thing).

Now, I don't mean for a moment to imply that such a tradeoff is necessarily bad—it may well be that it is, in fact, good, and that humanity would benefit more from broader and easier access to less research than from restricted access to more research. But it does seem to me that the question needs to be addressed rather than ignored or dismissed, and addressed in a rigorous, public, and aboveboard way. What I find worrying is rhetoric that seeks to prevent discussion of the question by implying that the tradeoff does not in fact exist—that funding dissemination as well as research involves no redirection of money from one to the other because the two are somehow inseparable. In the real world, you can't spend the same dollar on both research projects and dissemination, and this means that when funding agencies begin funding dissemination, they are inevitably going to end up funding less research. Proposing a new and more rhetorically convenient definition of "research" does not magically make this tradeoff disappear.

Pointing this out does not tend to endear one to those who are deeply invested in advancing the cause of OA at all costs. Those who resist dealing with this issue seem to see discussion of tradeoffs itself as an attack on the goals of OA. But the question is not whether more and freer access is a good thing; of course it is. The question—and I believe it is an urgent one—is this: Does the world benefit more from free access to $37 million less research or from restricted access to $37 million more research?

I don't pretend to have a universal answer to that question, nor do I assume that the answer will be the same for every type of research. What I do know is this: Playing word games in order to hide the reality of a tradeoff does not make the tradeoff go away. It only prevents rational and thoughtful decision-making, and if there's one thing the world of scholarly communication needs right now, it's more, not less, rational and thoughtful decision-making.

NOTES

1. Alliance for Taxpayer Access—American taxpayers are entitled to the research they've paid for, http://taxpayeraccess.org; Organisation for Economic Co-operation and Development, "Governments Should Improve Access to Publicly Funded Research, Finds OECD Report" (September 22, 2005), www.oecd.org/internet/governmentsshouldimp roveaccesstopubliclyfundedresearchfindsoecdreport.htm; International Coalition of Library Consortia, "New York State Higher Education Initiative" (June 14, 2012), http://icolc.net/consortia/83.

2. *Wikipedia*, "Serials Crisis," https://en.wikipedia.org/wiki/Serials_crisis.

3. For discussion of the various manifestations of this unwillingness, see essay 32 of this volume.

4. Robert Kiley, "Open Access at the Wellcome Trust: 5-Years On" (presentation at the Berlin 8 Open Access Conference, Beijing, China, October 25, 2010), www.slideshare.net/rkiley100/berlin8-kiley-oct10.

5. LISTSERV message archived at http://lists.ala.org/sympa/arc/ scholcomm/2011-08/msg00020.html.

6. Wellcome Trust, "The Reckoning: An Analysis of Wellcome Trust Open Access Spend 2013–14" (March 3, 2015), http://blog.wellcome. ac.uk/2015/03/03/the-reckoning-an-analysis-of-wellcome-trust- open-access-spend-2013-14; National Institutes of Health, "Policy on Enhancing Public Access to Archived Publications Resulting from NIH- Funded Research" (final policy statement, effective May 2, 2005), http:// grants.nih.gov/grants/guide/notice-files/NOT-OD-05-022.html#ftn8.

35

CC BY and Its Discontents

A Growing Challenge for Open Access

IN EARLY 2015, I attended the conference of a major learned society in the humanities. I was there for only a day and attended only two sessions: one as a panelist and the other as an observer. Both sessions dealt with issues related to open access (OA), and in both of them, I was deeply taken aback by the degree to which the scholars in attendance—not universally, but by an overwhelming majority—expressed frustration and even outright anger at the OA community. The word "predatory" was actually used at one point—not in reference to rapacious publishers, but to OA advocates. That was pretty shocking.

Later that year, in a different meeting, I listened to a presentation by the executive director of another large and important scholarly society, this one in the social sciences. His presentation was in no way heated or angry, but he made it abundantly clear that among his organization's members there was deep dissatisfaction with significant aspects of the OA movement's then-current direction.

Many private conversations before and since, often with scholars who did not want to publicly express anything that might be construed as objection or resistance to OA, have only reinforced the messages I received in those meetings.

What is the nature of the concern? Why would these scholars and scientists—academics who value the sharing of knowledge and who want to see the benefits of scholarship spread as broadly as possible (and who presumably want to reach as many readers as possible)—object to OA?

This essay was originally published in *Academic Newswire*, February 19, 2015.

The answer is that they don't typically object to OA itself, and in my experience, many of them say so very explicitly in the context of voicing their concerns and frustration. What they object to is a particular parameter of OA as it is currently defined by a large and dominant segment of the OA community: the Creative Commons Attribution (CC BY) license, which is enshrined in what is now the closest thing to a canonical definition that OA has—the Berlin Declaration on Open Access. Now, the declaration does not use the term "Creative Commons" (CC licensing was a relatively new thing when the Berlin Declaration was being formulated), but it defines acceptable reuse licensing in terms that align exactly with those of CC BY:

> *Berlin Declaration*: "The author(s) and right holder(s) of [open-access] contributions grant(s) to all users a . . . license to copy, use, distribute, transmit and display the work publicly and to make and distribute derivative works, in any digital medium for any responsible purpose, subject to proper attribution of authorship."[1]
>
> *CC BY definition*: "This license lets others distribute, remix, tweak, and build upon your work, even commercially, as long as they credit you for the original creation."[2]

What this means is that according to the Berlin Declaration, what makes an article OA is not the fact that it can be accessed and read by everyone at no charge. In order to be considered OA, the article's content (and "all supplemental materials") must also be made publicly available for any kind of reuse, including commercial reuse, without the author's permission.

It's important to note that not everyone in the OA community agrees that CC BY, or its functional equivalent, is a necessary feature of true OA. Some distinguish between "gratis" OA (which makes an article free to read but leaves the author some or all of the traditional exclusive prerogatives provided by copyright law) and "libre" OA (which makes it reusable under CC BY terms) and are happy to consider both of them genuine forms of OA. Some prominent voices in the movement insist that CC BY should not be regarded as a sine qua non of OA, while others assert that there is no such thing as OA without CC BY.

So why does this issue amount to more than intramural squabbling over a controversy that will inevitably end up getting resolved internally at some point? Several aspects of this controversy make it noteworthy, and worth careful consideration on the part of anyone interested in the future of scholarly communication.

First of all, although there is squabbling among individuals in the OA community about whether CC BY should be enshrined in our definition of OA, highly influential institutions have taken significant steps to make that enshrinement more official. In addition to its functional inclusion in the terms of the Berlin Declaration, CC BY licensing is also publicly endorsed by the Scholarly Publishing and Academic Resources Coalition (SPARC) as "the standard terms for Open Access."[3] Both the Gates Foundation and the Ford Foundation require that all of their grant-funded projects and research be published under CC BY licenses.[4] The Public Library of Science (PLOS)—whose journals collectively published more than 30,000 articles per year, making it the undisputed 500-pound gorilla of OA publishing—does not allow its authors to use any license other than CC BY.[5] Nor does BioMed Central, another very important OA publisher, or its sister company Chemistry Central.[6] In the United Kingdom, the Research Councils UK (which funds roughly $4.5 billion of research each year) also generally requires the results of research it funds to be published under a CC BY license.[7] (If a funded author does not use RCUK block grant funding to cover an article publishing charge, then she may restrict commercial reuse of her work.)

Second of all, consider the findings of a 2014 survey taken by the publisher Taylor and Francis among its authors, who represent a broad spectrum of academic and scientific disciplines. That survey found that fully 65 percent of them consider the reuse terms of CC BY to be "unacceptable."[8]

All of this suggests an important question: Why do authors mind? The answer will vary from author to author, of course, but one of the most common concerns expressed has to do very specifically with commercial reuse. In one documented situation, several authors who had published with PLOS and BioMed Central were startled and outraged to see that their articles had been bundled, without their permission but in full compliance with the terms of CC BY, into a high-priced book published by Apple Academic Press.[9]

In my experience, many authors who would happily make their work freely available for noncommercial reuse, adaptation, remixing, performing, etc.—for whom, in fact, that kind of free and noncommercial reuse is a big part of what OA is all about—are not comfortable allowing all comers to reuse their work commercially without at least asking permission. The authors I have spoken with mostly tend to say the same thing: "We believe in openness and sharing, and we want our work to be as freely and widely available as possible. But if you're going to take my work and somehow sell access to it or otherwise use it to make money, you need to ask my permission first." Some would be willing to allow commercial use in a *non-profit* context without permission; others don't want any commercial reuse of any kind without their authorization. Not all of the authors who have published in OA outlets have been aware that this has meant doing so under CC BY, but the number of authors who have figured this out is growing quickly, with predictable results. (And then there's the growing question of whether it would be acceptable to require students to make their work available on an OA basis, including CC BY, as a condition of academic progress.)

So the question we in the scholarly community need to be asking ourselves is this: Where do we believe authors' rights should end and the public's right to access and reuse should begin? Does it make a difference whether the scholarship in question was supported with public funds? If so, does public funding give the public a moral right to read the results of that scholarship, or to read and reuse without any restriction, or to read and reuse with some restrictions? What if the scholarly product was not supported by public funding—should it be made freely available simply because it's scholarship and we don't want to commodify knowledge?

I don't know how this issue will end up being resolved. One thing does seem clear to me, however: if authors (in the aggregate) have anything to say about it, the future of OA is unlikely to include CC BY as a required feature. Of course, not everyone wants authors to have anything to say about it. That fact should prompt us to deep and serious reflection about what we think the limits of academic freedom ought to be.

NOTES

1. "Berlin Declaration on Open Access to Knowledge in the Sciences and Humanities" (October 22, 2003), http://openaccess.mpg.de/Berlin-Declaration.

2. Creative Commons, "About the Licenses," http://creativecommons.org/licenses.

3. SPARC, "Open Access," www.sparc.arl.org/issues/open-access.

4. Bill and Melinda Gates Foundation, "Bill and Melinda Gates Foundation Open Access Policy" (January 1, 2015), www.gatesfoundation.org/how-we-work/general-information/open-access-policy; Timothy Vollmer, "Ford Foundation to Require CC BY for All Grant-Funded Projects" (February 3, 2015), https://creativecommons.org/weblog/2015/02/03/44865#.

5.   PLOS, "Open Access," www.plos.org/open-access.

6.   BioMed Central, "Licence Agreement," www.biomedcentral.com/about/policies/licence-agreement.

7.   Research Councils UK, *RCUK Policy on Open Access and Supporting Guidance* (Research Councils UK, April 8, 2013), www.rcuk.ac.uk/RCUK-prod/assets/documents/documents/RCUKOpenAccessPolicy.pdf.

8.   Taylor and Francis Online, *2014, Open Access Survey: Examining the Changing Views of Taylor and Francis Authors* (Routledge/Taylor and Francis, June 2014), www.tandfonline.com/page/openaccess/opensurvey/2014.

9.   Rosie Redfield, "Apple Academic Press: Predatory Publisher of Scholarly Books," *RRResearch* (blog), July 20, 2013, http://rrresearch.fieldofscience.com/2013/07/apple-academic-press-predatory.html.

36

Deceptive Publishing

Why We Need a Blacklist, and
Some Suggestions on How to Do It Right

IN RECENT YEARS, there has been increasing attention paid to the problem of what has come to be called "predatory" publishing—the characteristics of which are outlined by librarian Jeffrey Beall in his *Scholarly Open Access* blog, which also serves as something of a clearinghouse for information about those that Beall considers to be "potential, possible, or probably" predators.[1]

Beall's List (as it's affectionately or, sometimes, derisively known) has, unsurprisingly enough, accrued controversy and attracted lawsuits; some of that controversy is discussed in essay 32 of this volume. But the controversy arises not only because of the criteria Beall applies, or his fairness in applying them; it arises also from the ambiguity of the term "predatory" (is predation really the unique domain of open-access publishing?) and from the question of whether "blacklists" like Beall's are a useful and appropriate tool.

Here I would like to address both of those questions, first, by proposing a possibly more precise and useful designation for the kinds of publishers we're talking about and, second, by defending the appropriateness and utility of blacklists.

The term I would like to propose as an alternative to "predatory" is "deceptive." Deception, it seems to me, is the common thread that binds all of the behaviors that are most commonly cited as "predatory" in journal publishing, and I think it's the most meaningful and appro-

---

This essay was originally published in *The Scholarly Kitchen* (blog), September 22, 2015.

priate criterion for placing a publisher on a blacklist. Furthermore, "deception" is (unlike "predation") a concept with a fairly clear and unambiguous meaning in this context.

Varieties of Deceptive Publishing

It seems to me that deceptive scholarly publishing currently has four major manifestations:

Phony journals. These are journals that falsely claim to offer to the reading public documents based on legitimate and dispassionate scientific or scholarly inquiry. Such journals may be made available on either a toll-access or an open-access basis. One notable example from a few years ago was the *Australasian Journal of Bone and Joint Medicine,* which was published by Elsevier and presented to the world as a journal of objective scholarship but was later revealed as a promotional sock puppet for a pharmaceutical company—one such journal among several, as it turned out.[2] Truly phony journals of this sort are relatively rare.

Pseudo-scholarly journals. These are journals that falsely claim to offer authors real and meaningful editorial services (usually including peer review) and/or credible impact credentialing (usually in the form of an Impact Factor) and falsely claim to offer readers rigorously vetted scientific or scholarly content. In this case, the content may or may not be real scholarship—but the journal itself is only pretending to provide the traditional services of peer review and editorial oversight. This is perhaps the largest category of deceptive publisher, and also one of the more controversial ones, since the line between dishonesty and simple ineptitude or organic mediocrity can be fuzzy. For this reason, it makes sense to exercise caution in ascribing deceptive intent to these journals; however, in many cases (such as journals that falsely claim to have an Impact Factor, that lie about their peer-review processes, or that falsely claim editorial board members), deceptive intent can be quite clear.

False-flag journals. These are scam operators that set up websites designed to trick the unwary into believing that they are submitting their work to legitimate existing journals—sometimes by "hijacking" the exact title of the real journal and sometimes by concocting a new title that varies from the legitimate one only very slightly.

Masqueraders. This looks like a variety of hijacking, except that there is no actual hijackee. In these cases, journals adopt titles designed to imply affiliation with a legitimate- and prestigious-sounding scholarly or scientific organization that does not actually exist. For example, a Masquerader journal might call itself the *American Medical Society Journal* or *Journal of the Royal Society of Physicians.*

Why a Blacklist?

The prospect of setting up a blacklist raises a number of difficult and important questions. Here are some of them, followed by my suggested answers:

Does it make more sense to talk about deceptive publishers or deceptive journals?

Focusing on the journal at the title level is probably the best general approach, since not all such journals are part of a suite of titles put forward by a publishing organization. However, it's also worthwhile to take note of publishers that have a pattern of putting out deceptive journals.

When we talk about "predatory" publishers, why do they seem always to be open-access publishers?

There are two reasons, I believe: First, because this kind of scam simply works best on an author-pays basis, and author-pays models are, for obvious reasons, more prevalent in the open access world than in the toll-access world. The second, I believe, is because Beall is the only person who has yet taken the initiative to create and manage a predatory-publishing blacklist, and Beall is a vocal opponent of the open-access movement, which he has publicly characterized as "really [being] about anti-corporatism" and accused of wanting to "deny the freedom of the press" to those it disagrees with, of "sacrific[ing] the academic futures of young scholars" on the altar of free access, and of "foster[ing] the creation of numerous predatory publishers."[3] There have indeed been deceptive and arguably "predatory" toll-access journals, and the only reason I can think of for their exclusion from Beall's List is his specific opposition to the OA movement. As important and useful as his list has been, a more credible and useful blacklist would, I think, have to include deceptive toll-access journals—and would have to be more transparently managed. (See further discussion of this point below.)

What's the difference between either an inept publisher or a legitimate publisher of low-quality content and a truly predatory or deceptive publisher?

The difference lies in the intent to deceive. Deceivers are doing more than just running their journals badly or failing to attract high-quality content. In some cases, they are lying about who they are and what they're doing; in others, they are promising to do or provide something in return for payment and then, once payment is received, not doing or providing what they promised. Some focus their deceptive practices on authors, some on readers, and some on both.

What about toll-access publishers that engage in predatory pricing?

While I think it's worth calling out publishers who, in our view, engage in unfair or unethical leveraging of their monopoly power in the marketplace, this seems to me like a very different problem from that of essentially deceptive publishing. It's also an issue that is clouded by the fact that raising prices is not, in itself, necessarily unethical (unlike deception, which is).

Is it actually helpful to identify and call out these publishers? Why do we need blacklists? Can't we just have whitelists (like the Directory of Open Access Journals)?

Whitelists are good and important, but they serve a very different purpose. For example, a publisher's absence from a whitelist doesn't necessarily signal to us that the publisher should be avoided. It may be that the publisher is completely legitimate but has not yet come to the attention of the whitelist's owners, or that it is basically honest but doesn't quite rise to whatever threshold of quality or integrity the whitelist has set for inclusion, or that it is still in the process of being considered for inclusion. The function of a blacklist is also important, but it's very different. Among other things, it acts as a check on the whitelist; consider, for example, the fact that just over 900 questionable journals were included in the Directory of Open Access Journals (currently the most reputable and well-known OA whitelist on the scene) until its housecleaning and criteria-tightening in early 2015. If Walt Crawford hadn't done the difficult work of identifying those titles (work that, let's remember, was made possible by Beall's List), at what point, if ever, would they have been discovered and subjected to close examination?[4]

Is anyone really fooled by these predatory publishers? Wouldn't any idiot recognize their phoniness immediately?

Apparently not, in light of the DOAJ's recent experience. Furthermore, it's not just about whether authors are being fooled; it's also about whether predatory publishers help authors to fool others. Consider this hypothetical but reasonable scenario, for example: An author is coming up for tenure review and needs a few more peer-reviewed, high-impact journal publications on his list in order to be given serious consideration. This situation creates for the candidate an incentive to go with a deceptive or predatory pseudo-scholarly journal in the full knowledge that it is not legitimate, gambling that his tenure committee will not go to the trouble of researching the legitimacy of every journal on his publication list. Remember that even if a deceptive journal has a transparently phony-looking website, it will still yield a citation that looks, to the tenure committee, perfectly legitimate and natural nestled among other equally legitimate-looking citations on a CV. A well-researched, fairly managed, and transparently maintained blacklist could make every tenure or hiring committee's work quite a bit easier.

Nor is the danger posed by deceptive publishers limited to the academic sphere. Journals that have the appearance of scholarly and scientific rigor but that in fact will publish whatever an author is willing to pay them to publish pose risks to the general population by giving the appearance of scientific support to crackpot pseudoscience. Does this really happen? It certainly does. (For a good example, see http://io9.gizmodo.com/i-fooled-millions-into-thinking-chocolate-helps-weight-1707251800.)

How to Do It Right?

So assuming that blacklists actually do make sense, how should a blacklist be run? What would a well-researched, fairly managed, and transparently maintained blacklist look like? Obviously, there are issues of fairness and accuracy here: if you're going to publicly accuse a publisher of presenting its products and services deceptively, you need to be able to back up your accusations and you need to be able to demonstrate that the criteria by which you're making your judgments are reasonable and are being applied consistently. To that end:

- Criteria for inclusion must be clear and public.
- Those criteria must be applied consistently to all publishers, regardless of business model.
- The specific reasons for a publisher's or journal's inclusion must be provided as part of its entry.

- There must be an appeal process, and the steps required for appeal and removal must be clear and public.
- Appeals must be addressed promptly, and when denied, the reasons for denial should be clear and public.
- When a journal is removed from the list, the fact of its removal and the reasons for it should be clear and public.
- When a journal has been added to the blacklist erroneously, the error should be publicly acknowledged and the list owner should take responsibility for the error.

Roadblocks

Are there roadblocks to the creation of such a blacklist? Yes, many. For one thing, it would be costly; the research required to set it up and (especially) to keep it running in a fair and transparent manner would be considerable.

For another thing, the politics of running such a list are and would continue to be fraught. The publishers designated as "deceptive" will, in some cases at least, get upset. Sometimes their objections will be well-founded and the list owner will have to back up and apologize. Furthermore, there are some in the scholarly communication world who, for whatever reasons, don't want deceptive publishing to be discussed. Sometimes these commenters become publicly abusive, so whoever owns and operates the blacklist will have to have patience and a thick skin.

Would the cost be worth the benefit? I suspect so. The big question is whether there exists an entity willing to invest what it would take both to undertake this important project and to maintain it consistently, fairly, and transparently.

NOTES

1.   Jeffrey Beall, *Scholarly Open Access—Critical analysis of scholarly open-access publishing* (blog) http://scholarlyoa.com.

2.   Bob Grant, "Merck Published Fake Journal," *The Scientist*, April 30, 2009, www.the-scientist.com/?articles.view/articleNo/27376/title/Merck-published-fake-journal.

3.   Jeffrey Beall, "The Open-Access Movement Is Not Really about Open Access," *tripleC* 11 (2013): 589–97.

4.   Walter Crawford, "Journals, 'Journals,' and Wannabes: Investigating the List," *Cites and Insights: Crawford at Large* 14 (July 2014): 1–24.

37

The NPR Model and the Financing of Scholarly Communication

ALL OF US ARE familiar with the National Public Radio model of financing. It works like this: in order to provide programming with a minimal amount of advertising, NPR affiliates make a twice-yearly appeal to their listeners for voluntary contributions, which they call "memberships." These pitches are excruciating to listen to, partly because they last for ten days and partly because they consist entirely of variations on a single theme: "You love our programming, and you've been enjoying it for free. If people like you don't contribute, we'll go out of business. If you want to stop feeling guilty, you'll have to pony up."

There are some very interesting things about this model, one of which is that the individual listener derives no direct external benefit from ponying up. The risk involved in failing to pony up—the risk, that is to say, that one will lose access to the desired content—is practically nil. Furthermore, ponying up changes nothing about the listener's experience. Pledging a contribution doesn't even make the pledge drive stop; pledge early or pledge late or pledge not at all, and the pledge drive will last just as long. What changes for the listener is the amount of guilt he or she feels while listening to it.

It's true, of course, that if NPR listeners were to refuse en masse to contribute to their stations' support, at least some of those stations would in fact go out of business. But contribution decisions are made by individuals, not by crowds, and the risk to any individual listener that his or her station will go out of business due to his or her refusal to pony up is exceedingly low—far too low to act as a serious motivation to

This essay was originally published in *The Scholarly Kitchen* (blog), August 9, 2012.

contribute. For that reason, among others, an exceedingly low number of NPR listeners do in fact voluntarily contribute.

What does this have to do with scholarly communication? Right now, not much. But recent developments suggest that it could come to have more relevance in the future.

Consider what happened some years ago with the *Stanford Encyclopedia of Philosophy*, a peer-reviewed, freely available online publication that is updated on an ongoing basis and published by Stanford University. The project was begun in 1995 and then became a full-fledged online publication in 1998, attracting grant funding from the National Endowment for the Humanities (NEH) and the National Science Foundation (NSF). Its ongoing support now comes from a combination of foundation funding and voluntary contributions made by academic libraries and consortia, with matching funds from the NEH. So like NPR and its affiliate stations, the *SEP* subsists on a blend of public money and end-user contributions.

Now consider what happened just a couple of years ago with the arXiv. Originally developed and housed at the Los Alamos National Laboratory (LANL), the high-energy physics preprint server was for many years supported by LANL staff and a combination of NSF and Department of Energy funding. But according to Paul Ginsparg, the arXiv's founder and developer, support for the project among senior staff at LANL was weak, and when he left for Cornell in 2001, he took the arXiv with him. For the next ten years, the arXiv was funded jointly by the Cornell University Library and the university's computing faculty; according to an article in *Nature*, the library director at the time estimated that "maintaining the basic archive service would cost Cornell as little as $150,000 annually"—while also noting that the library intended to invest in structural improvements for both authors and end users.[1]

Fast-forward to 2010, when Cornell announced a new business model for maintenance of the arXiv. According to a publicly released budget summary, the annual cost of maintaining the service was by this point roughly $420,000, and Cornell announced that it was implementing a new system of voluntary support according to a three-tiered model under which the top 100 institutional users of the service would be asked to contribute $4,000/year, and the least-active users $2,300/year. This model was intended to keep the doors open while Cornell pursued a more permanent structural solution, and in 2012, the library announced that the Simons Foundation had given it a $60,000 planning grant "to support the development of a governance model that will guide the arXiv's transition from an exclusive initiative of Cornell University Library to a collaboratively governed, community supported resource."[2]

The *SEP* and the arXiv both represent very interesting case studies. Do they suggest anything generalizable about the future of scholarly communication? Obviously, it's hard to say—but I'm willing to stick my neck out this far:

First, they suggest that such a model can work, given sufficient institutional support (especially in the early going), and given strong agreement in the marketplace with the provider's value proposition. The *SEP* is widely respected as a reference source and it makes obvious sense as an online publication. The arXiv had built an exceptionally strong constituency long before anyone began asking that constituency for money. Both initiatives benefited considerably from years of comfortable incubation in an institutional setting before being nudged out into the cold world of direct-appeal fund-raising.

Second, and more subtle, the experiences of the *SEP* and the arXiv also suggest that such a model is unlikely to become a very serious factor in the near future. How do they suggest this? By having been prominent examples of the model for years and failing to generate much in the way of imitators. If the model were intrinsically interesting, it seems to me that the successful examples of both the *SEP* and, more recently, the arXiv would have led to the creation of more similar initiatives than they have. The fact that this model remains unusual suggests that it may not solve a problem that is widely perceived as serious by stakeholders in the research community.

There is a third issue at work here, and it's a simple but perhaps also rather subtle one. Budgets are tight, and this means that academic libraries (major fund-raising targets for both the *SEP* and the arXiv) have to make very hard decisions. We don't have the option of supporting everything that deserves our support, and we have to be ready to answer hard questions about our use of university resources. As an administrator charged with using those resources wisely, I have to be prepared to answer questions like "What direct benefit does the university realize in exchange for the library's expenditure of $X?" In the cases of the *SEP* and the arXiv, the simple answer is "nothing." Our students and faculty get the same level of access regardless of our support, and there is little or no chance that our failure to donate to those initiatives will lead to their disappearance. This doesn't mean that we shouldn't donate (in fact, we do). It does, however, have to factor into our decisions about donating, and if current budget trends continue, it very well could result in the cessation of our support.

The bottom line, I think, is that the NPR model of funding for scholarly communication bears watching—but I don't see it becoming a major player in the landscape anytime soon.

NOTES

1.   Declan Butler, "Los Alamos Loses Physics Archive as Preprint Pioneer Heads East," *Nature* 412 (July 2001): 3–4.

2.   Fiona Patrick, Oya Y. Rieger, David Ruddy, and Simeon Warner, "arXiv Business Planning Update" (Cornell University Library, January 2012), http://arxiv.org/help/support/arxiv_busplan_Jan2012.

INDEX

RICK ANDERSON is associate dean for collections and scholarly communication in the J. Willard Marriott Library at the University of Utah. He earned his BS and MLIS degrees at Brigham Young University and has worked previously as a bibliographer for YBP, Inc.; as head acquisitions librarian for the University of North Carolina, Greensboro; and as director of resource acquisition at the University of Nevada, Reno. He serves on numerous editorial and advisory boards, is a regular contributor to *The Scholarly Kitchen* blog, and has been a regular contributor to *Library Journal*'s *Academic Newswire*. His book *Buying and Contracting for Resources and Services: A How-to-Do-It Manual for Librarians* was published in 2004 by Neal-Schuman. In 2005, Rick was identified by *Library Journal* as a "Mover & Shaker"—one of the "50 people shaping the future of libraries." In 2008, he was elected president of the North American Serials Interest Group, and he was named an ARL Research Library Leadership Fellow for 2009–2010. In 2013, Rick was the recipient of the HARRASSOWITZ Leadership in Library Acquisitions Award and was invited to give the Gould Distinguished Lecture on Technology and the Quality of Life at the University of Utah. In 2015, he was elected president of the Society for Scholarly Publishing. He is a popular speaker on subjects related to the future of scholarly communication and research libraries.